COLLECTING PHOTOGRAPHS

"Awoke in a kind of vision. It was like the Annunciation! Suddenly, I saw what photography could be. . . . A tremendous potent form of art."

—ANSEL ADAMS, Diary 1931

Landt & Lisl Dennis

COLLECTING PHOTOGRAPHS

A GUIDE TO THE NEW ART BOOM

A SUNRISE BOOK | E. P. DUTTON | NEW YORK

Library of Congress Cataloging in Publication Data
Dennis, Landt and Lisl
    Collecting photographs.
        "A Sunrise book."
        Bibliography: p.
        1.   Photographs—Collectors and collecting.
I.   Dennis, Lisl, joint author.   II.   Title.
TR6.5.D46   1977   770'.75   76-51256
ISBN 0-87690-236-0
ISBN 0-87690-237-9   pbk.

Published simultaneously in Canada by Clarke, Irwin & Company Limited,
Toronto and Vancouver

10   9   8   7   6   5   4   3   2   1

First Edition
Designed by Ann Gold

CONTENTS

first photography galleries . . . Nineteenth-century photographs hard
to find . . . Companies buy photographs . . . Museums increasingly
enter market . . . Avedon show—a turning point . . . Center for
Creative Photography . . . Insistence on "well-known" images.

Numerous books of photographs . . . Consider a darkroom course
Proliferation of photo galleries . . . Confidence in dealer . . .
Auctions . . . Different types of collectable photographs . . . Fashion
and Hollywood photographs . . . Commercial photographs . . .
Guy Bourdin and the new eroticism . . . Weegee the famous . . .
Specialization: key to future photo collecting.

What about the negative? . . . Printing . . . Prints by photographer
preferable . . . Forgeries and fakes . . . Limited edition portfolios
Collectors question portfolio practices.

Conservatorial procedures . . . Mounting and matting . . . Storage
Trustworthy restorers . . . Inadequate scientific data . . . Upcoming
guide to photographers' practices . . . Value of restoration.

Color: what is it? . . . Fugitive color . . . Musicians invent
Kodachrome . . . AGFA secrets become war booty . . . Most
indelible print type . . . Guarantees against fading . . . Optimum
conditions for color prints . . . Doubts about guarantees . . . Color

coupler versus dye transfer . . . Cibachrome, the newcomer . . .
Other color media fade, too . . . International Museum of Photography
takes the lead . . . Cold storage . . . Most collectable print type . . .
Criteria for collecting color . . . Aesthetic doubts about color . . .
New schools of color photography . . . Technical doubts about color.

7 | **Photography Prices Today and Tomorrow—**
What the Collector and the Investor Need to Know   169

Cameron album sold for $120,000 . . . Set of *Camera Works* sold for
$35,700 . . . Contemporary photographers' works rise in price . . .
Established names safest investment . . . Value of vintage prints . . .
Portfolios can be good investment . . . Books containing rare
photographs . . . *Steerage* sold for $4,500 . . . Photography offers
few authenticated records . . . Hard to consider photography a sure
investment . . . Photographs by young artists a good buy . . .
"Extras" add to value of photograph . . . Avoid inferior prints . . .
Hidden treasures . . . Edwin H. Land and the Polaroid . . .
Rinhart buys 400,000 photographs a year . . . Rules for investing in
art, including photographs.

Appendices

PREFACE

In today's art world, no one with serious intentions of collecting can afford to plead ignorance before the Court of Appeals. "Caveat emptor" was, is, and always will be the rule of astute art buying and investing. Art in the twentieth century because of its general increase in value has become much more than simply something decorative with which to increase the beauty of an apartment, a house, or an office. It can be a blue chip investment as well as a painting, a piece of sculpture, an oriental rug. Or a photograph—the subject of this guide.

The Year of the Photograph was 1976. Suddenly, the media woke up to the growing interest of private collectors, museum curators, and even corporations in owning photographs. *The Wall Street Journal, The Washington Post, Newsweek, New York, Artforum, Print Collector's Newsletter,* NBC's *Today Show*—one after another, newspapers, magazines, and television networks focused the nation's attention on the nearly 150-year-old art of the camera. "Why the Photography Market Is Booming." "Blow Up—the Story of Photography in Today's Art Market." "Photography Is No Longer a Minor Art." "Photo Print Boom!" The articles kept coming. Headlines grew larger.

It took twenty years for *Life* and *Look* to make the United States a nation of picture literates. Then, when these great photography magazines were gone, gallery owners slowly began to fill the void. No longer considered simply a nostalgic glimpse of the past or benign recording of the present, photographs can now, in fact, command many thousands of dollars. To many experts, prices today—especially when you consider that there continue to be many fine photographs available for $75 to $150— are still cheap.

Not as inexpensive as they once were, though. "We fought, bled, and died for years to get as much as $25 for one of our photographs," a top-ranking photographer bemoans. "Now the people who bought them are reaping enormous profits. It doesn't seem fair."

Pollock, Van Gogh, Da Vinci—they undoubtedly would feel the same way were they still alive to see the prices their works currently command when they're available. But it is a fact of any marketplace that much sought-after items in short supply rise in price. It's true with wheat, diamonds, real estate, and now it's become true about photographs as well.

No one can really afford to be oblivious to the inherent multiplier often a part of a well-chosen work of art. "There are a lot of people who say they buy art only because they like it. It sounds less commercially crass, for one thing. And it hurts a lot less if they've suffered a loss if they're forced to sell," a museum curator confides confidentially. Like many colleagues, he hesitates to talk openly of art as an investment. But he admits that most collectors suffer no such qualms. "When someone has bought well, whether he likes it or not, his possession will increase in value. And someday, someone will be faced with its resale—his children, maybe his grandchildren. No art collection is ever permanent. Even if he gives his art to a museum, it will have to be appraised for IRS purposes. So say what you will art *is* an investment, including photographs.

Interviews with numerous dealers, museum curators, critics, educators, and photographers themselves have proved that, as with any collecting process, buying photographs intelligently requires a step-by-step procedure —one that most people don't know. As a result, they are fearful of making mistakes. This fear can, in fact, hold back potential collectors who would really like to know how to begin to acquire photographs.

We hope that our book can begin to eliminate this hesitation and can help to build public confidence. We haven't tried to delve deeply into the fascinating history of the medium, or to get overwhelmingly technical. Instead, we've touched on the key issues that pertain today to starting a collection of photographs, whether one is a museum or corporate curator or a private individual.

It is our sincere wish that anyone who reads this book can afterward walk into a photography gallery or an auction house, or browse through photographs at a country flea market, and feel confident and competent enough to make a value judgment and decision whether or not to buy a certain image.

Many people will want to dig into the subject of photography a great deal further, of course. For more scholarly research, the bibliography in the back of this book should help those collectors know what titles to ask for. For the gallery-goer, we believe that our listing of photography galleries throughout the world is as complete as a publisher's deadline allows. Each month brings new dealers onto the scene.

Most important of all, we hope that readers will share our love for the photography medium, especially the work being done by contemporary artists. Through education, through a refinement of taste, collectors should branch out from the acknowledged masterpieces of the past to include the remarkable works of today. The exciting thing about collecting photographs is that some of the greatest talents are alive and working right now. Many will be the Great Masters of tomorrow. It is the astute collector who will find them.

We wish to thank the following photography lovers, many of whom devoted hours of patience, insight, and advice to us in the production of this book. Our gratitude goes to: Casey Allen, Jacqueline Brody, Peter Bunnell, A. D. Coleman, John Coplans, Scott Elliot, Susan Harder, Marvin Heiferman, Anne Horton, Paul Katz, Harry Lunn, Jane Mull, Weston Naef, Marge Nejkrug, Cusie Pfeifer, Davis Pratt, George Rinhart, Robert Schoelkopf, Carl Siembab, Sam Wagstaff, Ealan Wingate, Cortia Worth . . . and all the photographers who shared with us their points of view.

December, 1976   LANDT & LISL DENNIS
New York City

GLOSSARY

The following is a list of terms most often used by collectors and dealers:

Albumen Print—The most popular printing paper used from 1850 to 1890, albumen paper was coated with egg white. The Dresden Albumenizing Company in Germany, in fact, used over 60,000 eggs a day. Later sensitized with silver salts, albumen paper had a smoother surface and finer detail than calotypes. Albumen prints are, however, subject to fading and discoloration.

Ambrotype—Resembling the daguerreotype, the ambrotype was the American name for glass collodion positive prints. Secured on a piece of glass and not a piece of silvered copper plate, the ambrotype does not produce the reflective mirror effect of a daguerreotype.

Calotype—Sometimes called a "Talbotype," the calotype was invented in September, 1841, by William Henry Fox Talbot. It was the first photograph secured on paper and made with a paper negative. Briefly exposing photogenic drawing paper to light, Talbot produced a latent image, later developed by gallic acid. The only negative/positive process in use before 1851, calotype positives were made from the negative by contact printing in daylight (up to 90 minutes!) without development.

Carte-de-visite—A French invention, the carte-de-visite, patented in 1857, was a popular form of professional studio portraiture. Measuring about 2¼ by 3¾ inches, the small images were meant to replace traditional calling cards. Through the use of multilens cameras, studios could make up to eight exposures at a time on a single glass negative plate. They were quickly adapted as a mass-produced opportunity to own portraits of celebrities. In fact, a London carte-de-visite company took four dozen negatives of Prime Minister Palmerston in 1864 at one sitting in order to place thousands of Palmerston cartes on the market immediately. Four years earlier, 100,000 cartes-de-visite of Abraham Lincoln were distributed during his presidential campaign.

Combination Print—A photographic image produced by combining two or more negatives, the combination print was especially popular in England in the 1850s and 1860s, when H. P. Robinson and O. G. Rejlander were noteworthy practitioners. Today many contemporary photographers enjoy including this technique in their "darkroom manipulations."

Daguerreotype—Invented in France in 1839 by L. J. M. Daguerre, the daguerreotype produced an image on the silvered surface of a copper plate sensitized with iodine vapor. It was then developed with mercury vapor. A "unique" image because no negative existed, only one daguerreotype could be made at a time. Daguerreotyping was the rage on both sides of the Atlantic in the mid-1850s.

Gelatin Dry Plates—Mass-produced between about 1880 and 1920, they were sold presensitized to photographers on thin glass in different sizes. The convenience of gelatin dry plates made them enormously popular.

Gum Bichromates—The fashionable form of photography in the late nineteenth and early twentieth centuries, these images are usually romantic and soft-focus on heavy artist's drawing paper. Often colored by the artists themselves with emulsions that they made, gum bichromates frequently resemble etchings, aquatints, and watercolors.

Heliographs—Discovered in 1826 by Joseph-Nicéphore de Niépce, the process required a copper plate to be coated with silver and covered with a film of bitumen, then exposed to light in the camera for several hours to produce an image.

Stereoscopic Photographs—The result of taking two photographs from two viewpoints separated by the same distance as that between the human eyes, stereoscopic photographs give a three-dimensional visual impression of depth. When looking through a stereoscope, viewers during the Victorian era delighted in looking at celebrities, wartimes scenes, the American West, still lifes, and disasters. Popular in both Europe and the United States, "stereographs," as these photographs are frequently called, were produced by the hundreds of thousands.

Tintypes—Also called ferrotypes, these photographs were produced by the wet collodion process on black- or brown-enameled iron plate rather than glass negatives. An American invention in the mid-1850s, tintypes cost as little as 25 cents for four pictures from a single exposure. Enormously popular, tintypes were frequently colored by hand.

Wet Plates—Invented by Frederick Scott Archer in 1851, the new photography technique quickly overtook the calotype and daguerreotyping process. Coated with collodion containing potassium and other iodides then immersed in silver nitrates, glass plates were exposed while wet, then developed immediately. The heavy, thick plates were used by such photographers as Brady.

1 | "Let There Be Light"

A BRIEF SURVEY OF THE INVENTORS OF PHOTOGRAPHY AND THE ARTISTS

"It can be said with certainty . . . that photography has remained
for a century and a quarter one of the most radical, instructive,
disruptive, influential, problematic, and astonishing phenomena of
the modern epoch."

—JOHN SZARKOWSKI, Director, Department of Photography,
Museum of Modern Art, New York City

ONE OF PHOTOGRAPHY'S UNIQUE QUALITIES IS THE FACT THAT THE medium isn't all that "ancient." Unlike paintings, lithographs, glass, bronzes, enamels, or any of the other countless "collectable" categories of art, the camera and its craftsmen are relative newcomers. Not even 150 years have passed since the first process of capturing a real-life image by means of photography was announced to the world.

The "Camera Obscura"

Man's fascination with "photography" had begun a good deal earlier, however. Aware that if a small hole is made in a piece of paper in a window of a darkened room, an image of the scene outside will be projected inside onto an opposite wall, the Chinese wrote about the process in the fourth century B.C. Later, Alhazen, a first-century A.D. Arab scholar; Roger Bacon in the thirteenth century; and Leonardo da Vinci in the fifteenth century also commented on the phenomenon.

It was Leonardo, in fact, who first used the phrase *camera obscura,* "darkened room," to describe the scientific experiment. "From the images of illuminated objects passed through a round hole into a very dark room, if you receive them on a piece of white paper placed vertically in the room at some distance from the aperture," he wrote, "you'll see on the paper all these objects in their natural shapes and colors. They will be reduced in size, and upside down owing to the intersection of the rays at the aperture. If these images come from a face that is illuminated by the sun, they will seem as if painted on paper, which must be very thin and viewed from the back."

Of great use to artists in copying nature with fine perspective by tracing the reflected image with brushes or pencils, the camera obscura process by the beginning of the nineteenth century reached the stage where there were three models to choose from. The most sophisticated was a portable box that reflected the image onto paper made translucent by soaking it in oil.

There had to be a next step, though, and scientists realized the need for a method by which the image of the subject could be projected through the opening onto a light-sensitive material that would retain the image. While this advance was to take centuries, when it occurred it happened almost simultaneously in the minds of two Englishmen, Thomas Wedgwood (1771–1805) and William Henry Fox Talbot (1800–1877), as well as two Frenchmen, Joseph-Nicéphore Niépce (1765–1833) and Louis-Jacques Mandé Daguerre (1787–1851).

Thomas Wedgwood, son of Josiah, the famous potter, was the first of the two Englishmen to succeed. In 1802 Wedgwood successfully found a way to treat paper or leather with silver salts in order to sensitize it to light. Drawing an image on a plate of glass, or placing ferns or lace on it, then placing the glass on top of the sensitized material and exposing them to sunlight, Wedgwood produced an image. He wasn't successful, though, in "fixing" it. What he was instrumental in doing, however, was connecting the properties of light to those of silver nitrate.

Talbot and the Paper Negative

William Henry Fox Talbot, a Cambridge-trained scientist, turned to photography because of his own inadequacies as a Sunday painter. On a trip to Italy in 1833 with his portable *camera lucida,* a more advanced model of the camera obscura, he independently came up with the idea of trying to fix the reflected image by means of chemicals. Two years later, he produced a paper that, when soaked in sodium chloride (common table salt) and silver nitrate, then washed in a strong solution of potassium iodide, became a negative. From this he could make an infinite number of positives by placing fresh sensitized paper in contact with the negative and exposing them to light.

Talbot's paper negative, the earliest in existence, of a window in his home, Lacock Abbey, in Wiltshire, can be seen today at the Science Museum in London. Patented as the *calotype,* Talbot's process is best studied in his book *The Pencil of Nature.* Published in 1844, it is one of the best-known, most-sought-after early photographic books in the world. With thirty-four calotypes of still lifes, architecture, and lace, it was, in fact, so startling in content that its publisher felt compelled to tell the world in an inserted slip that "the plates of the present work are impressed by light alone without any aid whatsoever from the artist's pencil."

The Invention of the Daguerreotype

On the other side of the English Channel, two Frenchmen, Joseph-Nicéphore Niépce and Louis-Jacques Mandé Daguerre, had also begun the hard work required to advance the science of photography. Having produced in 1826 the world's first photograph (the word was coined by the English astronomer Sir John Herschel in 1839) with an eight-hour exposure of his farmyard near Chalon-sur-Saône, Niépce joined forces in 1829 with Daguerre. A professional set designer who devoted so much time on the side to photographic experimentation that his wife thought he was going mad, Daguerre's major breakthrough occurred through happenstance. Working with silver coated copper plates rather than paper to retain the photographic image, he returned a plate to his chemical cabinet one night. It had been improperly exposed and he intended to repolish it. However, to Daguerre's astonishment the next morning, the latent image had been revealed. He repeated the process, and once more the mysterious secret of the copper plate was unveiled.

What had happened, he realized, was that the mercury vapors in his chemical closet had acted on the image of his underexposed plate. Continuing to work with Niépce, Daguerre labored more diligently than ever to understand "the spontaneous action of light." On Niépce's death in 1833, Daguerre was forced to work alone to perfect his method of photography: sensitizing a polished copper plate with silver and iodine vapor, exposing it in a camera, developing it with mercury vapor, and finally fixing the image with a common salt solution. Satisfied by 1839 that his improved results could be released to the public, Daguerre and Niépce's son sold their rights to what became known as the daguerreotyping process to the French government for a 6,000-franc annuity each. Subsequently, Daguerre's book *An Historical and Descriptive Account of the Various Processes of the Daguerreotype and the Diorama* became a best seller with more than thirty editions published in thirty languages throughout the world.

To Talbot and Daguerre photography therefore owes the origins of the two primary processes that have made its popularity so vast. While Daguerre's invention allowed photographers a way to develop the latent image after the copper plate had been exposed, Talbot's process, that of the negative/positive principle found in modern photography, permitted the printing of any number of images from a single negative. Of warmer, more flattering tones, Talbot's calotypes did not, however, have the precision of detail so much a part of the daguerreotypes. Needing to be held in such a way that the light did not reflect off the copper plates and hide the image, the daguerreotype was, nevertheless, a boon to artists seeking a shortcut to creativity.

No longer did students have to spend years in school learning how to draw, mastering the laws of linear perspective. Made available to the

---

WILLIAM HENRY FOX TALBOT (1800–1877). Calotype from *The Pencil of Nature,* 1844 (Graphics International, Ltd./Lunn Gallery).

Talbot was the first to take a negative-positive photograph. His works, among the earliest examples of the photographic medium, are eagerly sought by collectors.

world at large by the French government, the daguerreotype caught the public's fancy almost immediately—despite its continuing drawbacks! Only able to produce one image at a time (a real "plus" to today's collector, however, because of the undisputed uniqueness of each image), the new invention initially required the subject to remain immobile for between fifteen and thirty minutes. The slightest movement caused a blur on the copper plate. In 1840 the daguerreotype's next major advance occurred when England's John Goddard (1795–1866) cut down the exposure time to two minutes in summer and three to five minutes in winter, depending on the brightness of the sunlight.

Photography Spreads like Brushfire

From then on, the photography boom began. Like now, travelers were major camera fans. Returning from Egypt, Greece, and Israel, they brought with them captured likenesses of the Sphinx and the Parthenon. But more important to many of today's collectors was the work done by photography portraitists. The first public photographic studio in Europe was opened on the roof of the Royal Polytechnic Institution in London on March 23, 1841, by Richard Beard. The resulting excitement caused by having one's image taken by the "sacred radiance of the Sun" brought a never-ending stream of clients.

It was the phenomenal ability of the daguerreotype to reproduce the exact likeness of one's husband, one's lover, or even oneself that was such an essential part of the camera's magic and that caused its use to spread like brushfire throughout the world. Writing to a friend, the poet Elizabeth Barrett said: "It is not merely the likeness which is precious— but the association and the sense of nearness involved in the thing . . . the fact of the very shadow of the person lying there fixed for ever! . . . I would rather have a memorial of one I dearly loved, than the noblest artist's work ever produced."

The French artist Paul Delaroche, on examining a daguerreotype for the first time, expressed this sentiment himself when he said: "From today, painting is dead." Queen Victoria's court painter, Alfred Chalon, was more optimistic about the profession's continuation, though. When

UNKNOWN. *Edgar Allen Poe,* Daguerreotype, ca. 1848 (Helios Gallery).
Invented by Louis Jacques Mandé Daguerre in 1839, the daguerreotype process boomed. Today, prices for rare photographs of famous people have done the same. This image of Edgar Allen Poe sold for over $30,000 in 1976.

---

asked by the young queen if he did not think the new photographic process might eclipse his clients' enthusiasm for the canvas and brush, he was quick to respond in the negative. "Ah, non, madame! La photographie cannot flattère," he is reported to have said.

Still, men, women, and children delighted in the chance to be photographed, often for as little as twelve and a half cents. And nowhere was the public more quick to respond to daguerreotyping than in the United States. In fact, it was the American Samuel F. B. Morse (1791–1872) who persuaded the members of the new nation's National Academy of Design, composed mostly of painters, to appoint Daguerre an honorary member, a true act of turning the other cheek.

With their faces whitened by flour and often forced to sit under a sweltering sun, both the famous and "subjects unknown" sat down day after day to be photographed. By 1850 it was recorded that New York City alone had over seventy daguerreotype studios, with hundreds of others scattered throughout the country, as well as countless itinerant, often anonymous, photographers working the hinterlands. "It's no uncommon thing to find watch repairers, dentists, and other styles of business folk carrying on this 'Daguerreotyping' on the side," a writer of the age reported. "I have known blacksmiths and cobblers to double up with it, so it was possible to have a horse shod, your boots patched, a tooth pulled, and a likeness taken by the same man. Verily, a Daguerreotype man played many parts."

Mathew Brady, ". . . the First to Make Photography the Clio of War"

None achieved greater prominence than Mathew Brady (1823–1896). Owner of prosperous photographic portrait galleries both in New York and in Washington, D.C., he gained his permanent fame by recording the horrors of the American Civil War. A firm believer that "the camera is the eye of history," Brady and a team of employees sloshed through the blood and mud along with the Yankee troops. The civil war photographer's staff included Alexander Gardner (1821–1882), whose own *Photographic Sketch Book of the* [Civil] *War,* 1866, has become a valuable collector's item, and Timothy H. O'Sullivan (1840–1882), who later helped to photograph the American West.

The team's devotion to documentary photography enthralled *The New York Times* to such an extent that on July 21, 1862, it was reported that Brady was "the first to make Photography the Clio of war. . . . His artists have accompanied the army on nearly all its marches, planting their sun batteries by the side of our General's more deathful ones, and 'taking' towns, cities, and forts with much less noise, and vastly more

MATHEW BRADY (1823–1896). *Flag of the 8th Penna. Regiment,* ca. 1866 (Collection of the National Archives).

Commanding a staff of photographers, Brady documented the American Civil War. Because his name is stamped on every image, it is difficult to know whether Brady or an employee, including Alexander Gardner, took the photograph.

---

expedition. The result is a series of pictures christened 'Incidents of War,' and nearly as interesting as the war itself: for they constitute the history of it, and appeal directly to the great throbbing hearts of the North."

Later, on October 20, 1862, the *Times* continued its praise of Brady and his co-workers. This time the paper wrote that "Mr. Brady has done something to bring home to us the terrible reality and earnestness of war. If he has not brought home bodies and laid them on our dooryards and along the streets, he has done something very much like it. . . . It seems somewhat singular that the same sun that looked down on the faces of the slain, blistering them, blotting out from the bodies all semblance of humanity, and hastening corruption, should have thus caught their features upon canvas, and given them perpetuity for ever. But it has."

Boston's Famous Daguerreotypists: Southworth and Hawes

In Boston a team of photographers was to achieve acclaim as well. There Albert Southworth (1811–1894), a druggist, and Josiah Hawes (1808–1901), a journeyman carpenter, joined forces in 1843 to open a daguerreotype studio at 5½ Tremont Street. Almost immediately, the two men were recognized 'for their exciting new approach to their profession. Reducing the sitting time of a subject to only thirty seconds, they let it be known that they felt "Nature is not all to be represented as it is, but as it ought to be, and might possibly have been; and it is required of and should be the aim of the artist-photographer to produce in the likeness the best possible character and finest expression of which that particular face or figure could ever have been capable."

The statement was far too compelling for Ralph Waldo Emerson, Charles Goodyear, Harriet Beecher Stowe, Longfellow, and even Lola Montez—a cigarette firmly and defiantly held between her fingers—to resist. Here was a chance to show off one's best side. Determined to go "beyond the discovery and knowledge of the facts . . . [to] create and invent truths and produce new developments of facts," Southworth and Hawes are felt by some critics to have produced the finest portraits ever made by the daguerreotype process. Their aversion to stereotyped lighting and standard artificially theatrical poses reflected their subjects as true to life rather than stiff as a board.

The Advance of Photography in Europe

Still, European photographers weren't to be outranked by the Americans. Progress continued steadily in Britain in the mid-1850s, a period when

ALBERT SANDS SOUTHWORTH and JOSIAH JOHNSON HAWES (1811–1894 and 1808–1901). *Lola Montez,* ca. 1850 (Collection of the Metropolitan Museum of Art).

Southworth and Hawes became partners in 1841 in a Boston photography portrait studio. Considered among the nation's finest daguerreotypists, they recorded the faces of many famous personalities of their day.

photography was so much a part of the public awareness that the East India Company included it as basic training for its cadets. At the same time, however, there was a building resentment against photography by devoted painting fans. "There is no poetry in the pencil of the Sun," Sir David Brewster told readers of *The Journal of the Photographic Society* in May, 1856. "The photographer cannot separate what is beautiful from what is common . . . the painter and the sculptor have at their command resources of analysis and combination, selecting what is beautiful, suppressing what is offensive. . . ."

But photographers, undaunted, carried on. Talbot had by now improved his calotype process to the point where he estimated that only one sixtieth of the previous exposure time was now needed. Among the first to take advantage of this improvement were David Octavius Hill (1802–1870), a Scottish landscape painter, and Robert Adamson (1821–1848), an Edinburgh photographer. Asked to paint a convention of over four hundred Scottish Protestant ministers at Canonmills, Hill turned to Adamson for help. Together, in the years to come, they not only recorded the faces of the ministers, translated twenty-three years later into a 5-by-12-foot canvas, but photographed other people from all walks of life as well. Adamson was responsible for the technology, Hill for the posing of his sitters. The result was one of the world's most spontaneous genre photography teams.

Frederick Archer (1813–1857) was another important contributor to the process of the photography medium. He added his name to history by inventing the wet-plate, or collodion, process in 1851. Employing a glass negative able to record precise details, from which quantities of paper prints could be made, the new technique was used in the United States to produce imitation daguerreotypes called *ambrotypes.* Another variation resulted in *tintypes,* in which photographers used thin black-enameled iron sheets coated with collodion emulsions rather than glass negatives.

Photographers Faced Horrendous Complexities

Still, despite improvements, photographers continued to face horrendous complexities when shooting a picture. Not only did the wet plates demand immediate use, but rapid developing was necessary. For on-the-scene documentation, cumbersome darkrooms had to be lugged to mountain plateaus and inside combat zones. America's Mathew Brady had faced this problem, and so did England's Roger Fenton (1819–1869), who recorded the Crimean War.

For some artists it wasn't quite so bad, though. Especially when you had as many assistants as surrounded Parisian caricaturist Gaspard Félix Tournachon, better known professionally as Nadar (1820–1910). The artist turned to photography in 1853 in order to record a large number of prominent Frenchmen for his caricature lithograph the "Panthéon Nadar," and his passion for plain backgrounds and diffused light to bring out details in both his subject's face and his dress drew the city's aristocracy, intelligentsia, and society through his doors.

The list included Delacroix, Daumier, Victor Hugo, and George Sand, as well as the most prominent officials of both the Second Empire and the Third Republic, all of whom rushed off to be preserved for posterity by Nadar.

Later, when the Impressionists were looking for a place to show their works for the first time, the French photographer welcomed them into his old studio, from which he had recently moved. The publicity directed to the renegade painters spilled over to Nadar as well, and business increased for him still more!

Julia Margaret Cameron's "Divine Art"

Julia Margaret Cameron (1815–1879), a Scottish gentlewoman whose daughter had given her a camera in order to relieve her boredom, proved equally as aggressive and adept behind a camera. Despairing of shallow photography, which she said failed to reveal "the greatness of the inner as well as the features of the outer man," she excelled in what is known today as the close-up. Blessed with financial independence but bedeviled by a compelling fascination for the "divine art" of photography, Mrs. Cameron badgered everyone within earshot to pose for her. No sooner had she finished pouring them a cup of tea than she would steer her victims to the front of her camera and compel them to remain immobilized

NADAR (1820–1910). *George Sand,* 1864 (Collection of the Metropolitan Museum of Art).

Nadar, or Gaspard Félix Tournachon, could be called the Grand Master of photographic portraiture. Curiously, though, he refused to photograph women. The only exceptions to this rule were Sarah Bernhardt and George Sand.

while she went to work to record their face. Tennyson, Carlyle, Browning, and Darwin were among the great lady's hostages.

The famous Italian military leader Giuseppe Garibaldi avoided the photographer's advances, however. Hearing that he was staying with a neighbor, Alfred, Lord Tennyson, Mrs. Cameron bundled up her camera gear and hurried into the garden where the general was sunning himself. Surprised, not knowing who the aggressive *paparazza* was, Garibaldi uttered the command to retreat. Mrs. Cameron did, miffed no doubt, but still undaunted. Frustrated a while later by Crown Prince Frederick of Prussia's inability to hold his head up high while she labored behind her camera, Julia Margaret seethed with frustration and fury. "Big eyes! Big eyes!" she hollered, no doubt raising the royal blood to the boiling point.

A devotee of subdued lighting, which forced her subjects to hold still anywhere from four to six minutes, Mrs. Cameron was especially fond of allegorical studies of children and young people, dressed in classical costumes and acting out biblical passages. Still, the command to "do unto others as you would have them do unto you" failed to register.

One young lady who fell under the famous photographer's spell recalled the excruciating pain of it all. "The studio . . . was very untidy and very uncomfortable," she recorded years later. "Mrs. Cameron put a crown on my head and posed me as the heroic queen [Zenobia]. This was somewhat tedious, but not half so bad as the exposure. Mrs. Cameron warned me before it commenced that it would take a long time, adding, with a sort of half groan, that it was the sole difficulty she had to contend with in working with large plates. . . . The exposure began. A minute went over and I felt as if I must scream; another minute, and the sensation was as if my eyes were coming out of my head; a third, and the back of my neck appeared to be afflicted with palsy; a fourth, and the crown, which was too large, began to slip down my forehead; a fifth —but here I utterly broke down, for Mr. Cameron, who was very aged, and had unconquerable fits of hilarity which always came in the wrong places, began to laugh audibly, and this was too much for my self-possession, and I was obliged to join the dear old gentleman. When Mrs. Cameron . . . bore off the gigantic dark slide with the remark that

JULIA MARGARET CAMERON (1815–1879). *Madonna,* ca. 1865 (Graphics International, Ltd./Lunn Gallery).

A "grande dame" of early photography, Cameron was charming, caustic, despotic, and relentless. She pursued the famous and the unknown with her camera. Everyone *had* to pose for her, for hours. Today, her images are sought by museums and collectors at high prices.

---

she was afraid I had moved, I was obliged to tell her . . . I had." *

Insistent that the photographs she obtained were the "embodiment of prayers" (which they are today to collectors, since they continue to skyrocket in value), Mrs. Cameron, and the other camera enthusiasts in the second half of the nineteenth century, frequently found themselves no

* Editors of Time-Life Books, *The Camera,* Life Library of Photography (New York: Time-Life Books, 1970), pp. 177–178.

less the subjects of persecution than the ancient Israelites. Perhaps part of the problem was the as-yet-undefined answer to what "art" should be and, therefore, to whether photography had a right to be included in the definition. The miniature painter Sir William Newton (1785–1869), for instance, insisted that photography was merely an adjunct to painting. But one which, nevertheless, could be useful to painters, provided the photographs were taken "in accordance (as far as it is possible) with the acknowledged principles of Fine Art." One way that this could be done, Newton said, was to make certain that the photograph was slightly out of focus, a practice that was to linger for many years.

Rejlander and the Multi-negative Process

Other critics added that the photograph might be judged on its own artistic merits *provided* it was produced with the same exaggeration and flamboyance so much a part of contemporary theater, an *a priori* rule that frequently demanded the use of several negatives to produce one print. Oscar G. Rejlander (1813–1875), for instance, required thirty negatives for the final print of his allegorical image *The Two Ways of Life,* a depiction of Industry and Dissipation. As large as an easel painting, 16 by 31 inches, and hung beside paintings, drawings, and sculpture in the Manchester Art Treasures Exhibition in 1857, the photograph enthralled the critics and enchanted Queen Victoria. Paying a modest ten guineas, she bought it for her husband, Prince Albert, making the photograph one of the first to be purchased by a recognized patron of the arts.

The Scots had not been nearly so open-minded about *The Two Ways of Life,* though. When the photograph had hung in Edinburgh, only half of it was shown. The nude portion was carefully concealed behind drapery!

Another manipulator of photographic negatives at this time was Henry Peach Robinson (1830–1901). If a particular scene did not work out, simply recompose it in the darkroom, he counseled. If the garden background behind a milkmaid was not right, take the girl out of the garden and superimpose her on top of another one. A strong advocate of the "pictorial photography" method whereby you built up a negative by stages, Robinson's book on the subject, *Picture Making by Photography,* was still in print, remarkably enough, after World War I. "Any dodge, trick, and conjuration at any time is open to the photographer's use . . ." he wrote. "It is his imperative duty to avoid the mean, the bare, and the ugly, and to aim to elevate his subject, to avoid awkward forms and to correct the unpicturesque."

Peter Henry Emerson (1856–1936) didn't agree. A physician by profession, but an ardent amateur photographer, Emerson blasted Robinson's artificiality and campaigned vigorously for what today is considered to be "straight photography." In the hands of a talented artist, the camera should be used without artificial lighting to record natural scenes, real people, and actual events, Emerson insisted. Photographers should respect the photographic process and limit their controls to those inherent to the tools of the trade, he said.

Photographers Delight in the American West

An admirer of the Barbizon School of painting, especially Millet, Emerson delighted in depicting the life and landscape of England's Norfolk Broads—no more so, though, than American photographers Timothy O'Sullivan and William Henry Jackson (1843–1942) thrilled to the scenes of the American West through their own lenses. Crossing the plains in a covered wagon and setting up a photography studio in Omaha, Nebraska, in 1868, Jackson was commissioned by the Union Pacific Railroad to produce a series of images to promote the spectacular landscape through which the new rails ran. Later he was commissioned to record the Yellowstone area by F. V. Hayden, a geologist hired by the government to survey it.

Congress, influenced by Jackson's photographs, created Yellowstone National Park.

O'Sullivan, in 1867–1879, was also employed by the government. In his case, it was to record the nation's Fortieth Parallel, a documentation that continues to enchant collectors with the photographer's large, powerful images of the Colorado River and the Canyon de Chelly in Arizona.

TIMOTHY O'SULLIVAN (1840–1882). *Carson Desert, Nevada,* c. 1868 (Collection of the Library of Congress).

Official photographer of the U.S. Geological Exploration of the Fortieth Parallel, 1868–1869, O'Sullivan recorded the expedition's portable ambulance, which doubled as his own portable darkroom. O'Sullivan's Western photographs are considered among the finest. Their large size adds to the frontier's monumentality.

Other photographers who literally turned photography into a universal art during this time, and whom collectors and museums now favor, include Francis Frith (1822–1899), an Englishman, mesmerized by Egypt; Felice Beato, another Briton, who was enthralled by India; and America's John Dunmore, who returned home with scenes of icebergs and Eskimos in Greenland.

WILLIAM HENRY JACKSON (1843–1942). *Crater of the Grand Geyser,* 1872 (Sotheby Parke Bernet, Inc.).

Jackson was the official photographer of the U.S. Geological Survey Territories. Often called "the grand old man of the National Parks," his photographs of the American West confirmed explorers' descriptions of the grandeur of the Tetons, Rocky Mt. National Park, and Yellowstone. It was his photographs that convinced Congress to turn Yellowstone into a National Park. One could say that Jackson early demonstrated that photography can help bring about greater environmental appreciation, social change, and the like.

Popularity of Stereographs and Cartes-de-Visite

Also of growing appeal to photograph collectors today are the stereographs that all of these men, and many thousands of others, took. Double pictures, taken with a twin-lens camera, they were able to produce a remarkable three-dimensional effect when seen through a viewer. Normally 7 by 3½ inches when mounted, the twin photographs, separated by about 2 inches, quickly became the rage, especially after Oliver Wendell Holmes (1809–1894) invented a simple aluminum eyepiece that could be adjusted for sharp focusing. In the years before newspaper reproduction of photographs, it is estimated that millions of stereographs were produced for a public hungering after visual education and amusement.

Another contemporary craze at that time stemmed from André Disdéri's (1819–1890) technique of producing eight photographs on one plate. Known as "cartes-de-visite" because of their small size, about the same as calling cards of the day, the miniature portraits became an overnight sensation, triggered by the vanity of Napoleon III. On his way out of Paris in 1859 leading an army headed for Italy, the emperor halted his troops for a few minutes in front of Disdéri's studio on the Boulevard des Italiens and rushed inside for immortalization. Within two years the Parisian photographer's business made him one of the wealthiest practi-

---

GEORGE CURTIS. *Niagara Falls,* ca. 1875 (Collection of the Metropolitan Museum of Art).

An inexpensive, mass-produced form of early "entertainment," stereographs are rapidly becoming discovered by collectors. The result? Stereograph prices are rising.

30 American Fall and Ice Mountain

MESSIER, PHOT.

MESSIER. *Carte-de-Visite of Priest,* ca. 1890 (Collection of the authors).

Cartes-de-visite are found in antique and junk shops today. Intended to replace calling cards, they were produced by the millions in Europe and the U.S. Frequently they were taken by little-known photographers of anonymous subjects—neither of which takes away from the images' fascination.

---

tioners of the art in Europe, with additional studios in Toulon, Madrid, and London.

J. J. E. Mayall, who had taken "cartes" of Queen Victoria and the Prince Consort in May, 1860, also helped to fan the flames of the new craze. With both the French and the British royalties' stamps of approval, "cartomania" accelerated at a breathtaking speed. People competed fiercely to include in their "carte albums" images of famous personalities as well as of their own family members.

With the introduction of this even less expensive way of photography than the daguerreotype to show one's grandchildren what one looked like, photography reached out to a larger mass market than ever before. Speaking of the carte-de-visite process as "the people's art," London's *Photographic News* reported in 1861 that "photographic portraiture is the best feature of the fine arts for the millions that the ingenuity of man has yet devised. It has in this sense swept away many of the illiberal distinctions of rank and wealth, so that the poor man who possesses but a few shillings can command as perfect a lifelike portrait of his wife or children as Sir Thomas Lawrence painted for the most distinguished sovereigns of Europe."

Gelatin Plates Spur "Instant Photography"

An extraordinary new process developed by an English physician, Richard Leach Maddox (1816–1902), in 1871, stepped up photography's momentum still more. Experimenting with a gelatin silver bromide emulsion as a substitute for collodion on glass plates before exposure, Maddox offered the first step in a process whereby photographers could be free from having to make their own plates, or having to develop them immediately afterward. Even more important, the new gelatin dry plates were more sensitive than the old wet plates, thereby allowing exposures to be made in a fraction of a second.

Soon factories began to mass-produce the new plates and photography took a new turn. Action shots now became a great deal more popular, an evolution spurred on by America's Eadweard Muybridge (1830–1904). The inventor of "instantaneous photography," Muybridge was commissioned by railroad millionaire Leland Stanford to prove that a horse raised all four feet simultaneously in the air when it ran—a fact unable to be seen by the naked eye, but a hunch on which Stanford had a $25,000 bet with a friend.

Setting up twelve different cameras at intervals of 27 inches to be set off at shutter speeds of 1/1000 second by black threads severed by a running horse, Muybridge's twelve photographs, taken by the wet-plate method, proved Stanford right and artists' traditional "rocking-horse" depictions to be wrong. Improving his technique considerably by shifting to the new gelatin-plate process, Muybridge, between 1872 and 1885,

went on to produce a body of work known as *Animal Locomotion*. A series of images showing both human as well as animal movement, the photographs were published by the University of Pennsylvania in 1887.

George Eastman and the Kodak Camera

Freeing the amateur from the need for a tripod because of their speed, the gelatin plates next led to the introduction of the hand-held camera. These cameras were known at first as "detective cameras" for their inconspicuousness, which allowed the owners to take candid shots without anyone knowing it. The most famous of the new line of equipment was the Kodak, the revolutionary idea of a young bank clerk in Rochester, New York, named George Eastman (1854–1932).

About to take a vacation in the Caribbean, Eastman had been urged by a friend to take along a "photographic outfit." The outfit, Eastman discovered, entailed a cartload of equipment, including a light-tight tent.

EADWEARD MUYBRIDGE (1830–1904)
Animal Locomotion, 717 The Cat., ca.
1884 (Martin Gordon, Ltd.).

Interested in movement, Muybridge was invited by the University of Pennsylvania to produce over 100,000 photographs of animals and humans in motion. Muybridge's experiments led the way to contemporary cinema photography.

It was cumbersome and hardly conducive to a relaxed holiday. So the young American abandoned his holiday plans and immediately set to work to improve the tedious process. He not only did, but, even more significant, he discovered a machine for making dry plates both uniformly and in quantity.

Taking out an American patent in 1880, George Eastman and his partner, Henry A. Strong, began the Eastman Dry Plate Company. Anxious to produce a roll of film such as we now know it, Eastman worked night and day. Again he succeeded. In 1884 he startled the world by announcing that "American Film" was now on sale. Weighing as much as a dozen glass plates but able to produce forty ⅘-inch negatives, the spool could be rolled up in a small area and was adaptable to almost every plate camera on the market.

Then, in 1888, Eastman came out with the Kodak, a light, portable instrument that could be easily packed by travelers and hand-held with ease. "I devised the name myself. . . . The letter 'K' had been a favorite with me—it seems a strong, incisive sort of letter," Eastman explained in 1920 to a reporter for *System* magazine. "It became a question of trying out a great number of combinations of letters that made words starting and ending with 'K.' The word 'Kodak' is the result."

Costing $25 and loaded with enough film to take 100 photographs, the little box's instructions read: "Pull the string. . . . Press the button. . . . Turn the key. . . ." This set the shutter, took the exposure, then wound fresh film onto the roll. Returning the camera to Rochester, where the film was removed and prints made, the owner could have a new roll inserted for another $10.

Millions did, spurred on by Eastman's even greater breakthrough, that of gelatin emulsion on clear, transparent material made of nitrocellulose. Renamed the Eastman Kodak Company, and determined to mass-produce its cameras and films to meet the ever-growing popularity of photography, the firm found an immediate market in the numerous camera clubs that quickly sprang up throughout the country.

Stieglitz: Founder of Photo-Secession

Of all the early-twentieth-century Americans who recognized photography's ability to be an effective means of artistic expression, none devoted himself to the task of demonstration with more skill and determination than Alfred Stieglitz (1864–1946). Awarded his first photography prize by none other than England's Peter Henry Emerson when he had shown his work in Europe, Stieglitz, American-born but educated in Germany, served as editor of the *American Amateur Photographer* magazine when he returned to the United States in 1890. Later he organized the Camera Club in New York and founded his own periodical, known as *Camera Notes and Proceedings.*

Stieglitz was a passionate devotee of the hand-held camera; so much so that his photographs of Manhattan frequently required him to stand still for hours until he felt the mood was exactly right to open the shutter. Whether he had been captivated by the sight of a train, a milk delivery wagon, or a building, whether he was caught in a snowstorm or bathed in a gentle spring shower, Stieglitz persevered. "When I see something that serves as an 'equivalent' for me of what I am experiencing myself, then I feel compelled to set down a picture of it as an honest statement—which statement may be said to represent my feelings about life," the photographer said.

Alarmed by the dangers of inconsequential snapshooting, he counseled readers in an article he wrote entitled "The Hand Camera—Its Present Importance" to "choose your subject, regardless of figures, and carefully study the lines and lighting. After having determined upon these, watch the passing figures and await the moment in which everything is in balance; that is, satisfies your eye. This often means hours of

---

ANONYMOUS. *American Newsboys,* Tintype, ca. 1860 (Collection of the authors).

A "poor man's" daguerreotype, tintypes cost as little as 25¢. Illustrations of people clothed in their occupational garb, holding the tools of their trade, are sought after by today's collector.

patient waiting. My picture, 'Fifth Avenue, Winter,' is the result of three hours' standing during a fierce snow storm on February 22, 1893, awaiting the proper moment."

Determined to legitimize photography, to promote the artistic capabilities of the camera, Stieglitz championed the work of other photographers of his time, including Edward Steichen (1879–1973), Clarence H. White (1871–1925), and Gertrude Käsebier (1852–1934). Forming the Photo-Secessionist movement, the purpose of which was to dignify the photography profession, which still battled the question of whether it was art or a trade, Stieglitz and his colleagues founded a new magazine, *Camera Work*. Containing extensive reviews and articles, the quarterly publication, begun in 1903 and ended in 1917, was one of the most beautiful photography magazines ever produced. So much is it valued, in fact, that in 1976 a complete set sold for $35,000, with individual images removed from its covers fetching into the high hundreds.

The Photo-Secessionists also had their own gallery. Known as 291 from its Fifth Avenue address, it achieved equivalent fame to that of its founders by showing the work of such additional avant-garde artists as Cézanne, Picasso, and Matisse. To Stieglitz, photography was a revolutionary art that could, and should, stand up beside other contemporary media. Isolation was something that photography did not need, he contended.

Publishing its own regular periodical, *291,* the gallery unknowingly contributed enormously to the current photography marketplace when it printed in one issue a handsome 11-by-14-inch photogravure of Stieglitz's photograph *The Steerage*. On a trip to Europe in 1907, the photographer was walking on the deck of a ship when he saw a group of emigrants down below. Hurrying to get his Graflex from his room, he said, he'd had a flash of inspiration at that moment. Later he wrote: ". . . a round straw hat, a funnel leaning left, the stairway leaning right, the white suspenders crossing on the back of a man in the steerage below, round shapes on iron machinery, a mast cutting into the sky . . . I saw a picture of shapes and underlying that, a feeling I had about life."

Worth many thousands of dollars today and continuing to command a higher and higher price, *The Steerage* photogravure exemplifies the philosophy of its creator, who had become a convert to the school of straight photography. Critic and scholar Beaumont Newhall explained this approach by saying that a photographer who practices this unadorned approach to his profession "finds almost instantaneously a certain moment of time which, frozen on film, will live forever. He must recognize the framework, not contrive a 'composition'; he must feel the emotional impact and he must have the ability to capture it with his techniques."

Strand—Forerunner of Straight Photography

Paul Strand (1890–1976), whose work was given a one-man show at the 291 gallery, was a prime trend-setter in this straight-photography movement, adding still another stage to the development of American photography. Fascinated by abstract patterns in nature, of New York traffic seen from above, of commonplace objects such as car wheels, bowls, and fences, also of "hurt, eroded people," Strand explained his approach to photography in an issue of *Camera Work*. He wrote: "Objectivity is the very essence of photography, its contribution and at the same time its limitation. . . . Honesty no less than intensity of vision is the prerequisite of a living expression. The fullest realization of this is accomplished without trick processes or manipulation, through the use of straight photogenic methods."

This new vision of photography in the 1920s was not, however, limited to New York. The concern had hit California as well. There the camps were divided between the Fuzzy-Wuzzies and the Sharp-and-Shinies, or the f/64 group. Led by William Mortensen, a Hollywood publicity photographer, the Fuzzy-Wuzzy movement felt the art of the camera should be ruggedly selective and follow the classic style. Mortensen wrote that "the final concern of art is not with facts, but with ideas and emotions." Imogen Cunningham (1883–1976), Edward Weston (1886–1958), and Ansel Adams (1902–   ) led the f/64 group, favoring a direct, realistic use of the camera. Adams, whose work is now sought the world over, wrote in an early essay entitled "What Is Photographic Beauty?" that "the photographer's power lies in his ability to create his subject in terms of its basic reality, and present this recreation in such a form that the spectator feels that he is seeing not just a symbol for the object but the thing itself revealed for the very first time." *

To this Weston added: "The camera should be used for a recording of *life,* for rendering the very substance and quintessence of the *thing itself,* whether it be polished steel or palpitating flesh." Using a sharp-cutting lens, well stopped down to ensure great depth of field and the complete avoidance of artificial lighting, he insisted that a photograph should "be sharply focused, clearly defined from edge to edge, from nearest object to most distant. It should have a smooth or glossy surface to better reveal the amazing textures and details to be found only in photographs. Its values should be clear cut, subtle or brilliant, never veiled." †

The Birth of Photojournalism

This new, bold approach to photography led right into photojournalism. The casual and incidental were no longer adequate, aggressive photographers in the early twentieth century insisted. The final image should exist in its completeness before the image was recorded, and the developed print should reveal the facts exactly as they were *when* the photographer released his camera shutter, they maintained.

In other words, let us take a long, hard, cold look at the world around us, photographers began to say . . . and do. Eugène Atget (1857–1927) had begun the process at the turn of the century in his native Paris. Daily recording the French capital's storefronts, street scenes, buildings, carrousels, the people who earned their living on the street, he went generally unrecognized until Man Ray (1890–1976), an American painter turned photographer and famous for his "rayograms," printed a few of Atget's images in the periodical *La Révolution Surréaliste* in 1926. Later, Atget's entire collection of prints and negatives was saved by American photographer Berenice Abbott. A noted photographer in

* Adams, Ansel, "What is Photographic Beauty?", *Camera Craft,* vol. XLVI, no. 61 (June, 1939), p. 254.

† Weston, Edward, *Enjoy Your Museum* (Pasadena, Calif.: Esto Publishing Company, 1934), p. 12.

her own right, she later sold them to the Museum of Modern Art in New York City.

Other Europeans who trained their eyes to see a significant event in the world around them in a split second and to record it with such artistry that it lasts forever included André Kertész (1894–), Henri Cartier-Bresson (1908–) and Brassaï (1899–). The latter wrote that the instantaneous approach that the photographer must demonstrate includes "keenness of power of observation; patience and hawk-like speed in swooping on his prey; impulsiveness; preference for the human race and indifference to mere faces of reality; spurning of colour and the enjoyment derived from the restraint and sobriety of black upon white; and, finally, a desire to get beyond the anecdotal and to promote subjects to the dignity of types."

Jacob Riis (1849–1914), a Dane by birth, an American by choice, carried this early-twentieth-century gut-level approach to photography directly into the appalling tenements, alleyways, and communal showers of New York's down-and-out Jewish, Italian, and Irish immigrants. Using his camera as well as his words as a means of propaganda, Riis, who worked for the *New York Tribune,* later the Associated Press, fought to improve the new arrivals' living and working conditions.

This documentary style of photography was added to later by Lewis Hine (1874–1940), a teacher at one time at Manhattan's Ethical Culture School and a trained sociologist. Distraught at the plight of the underprivileged caused by the effects of industrialization upon urban life, Hine said that he wanted to "show the things that had to be corrected" as he set about recording the lives of the poverty-stricken. His black and white evidence of the dreadful factory conditions where children as young as six years old were forced to work dangerous machinery in filthy, depressing surroundings helped spur Congress to pass legislation against child-labor abuses.

FSA Photographers—Symbol of Dedication

Later, in 1935, the U.S. government, through the auspices of the Farm Security Administration (FSA), called photographers to the cause of human concern in a time of crisis. Under Roy Stryker, FSA photographers were asked, with no deadlines, no editor dictating his own preferences, to record the plight of midwestern farmers driven from their land as the result of a four-year drought and the encroachment of big farming co-operatives. The beauty, the insight, the historic significance of these images have made them some of the most appreciated possessions in the hands of collectors and museums today. Dorothea Lange, Arthur Rothstein, Walker Evans, Ben Shahn, Carl Mydans: they all contributed to a body of work unique in the history of photography, a combination of compassion and creative genius.

Also adding to the documentation of America at this time was Margaret Bourke-White (1904–1971), who with her husband, Erskine Caldwell, published a sensitive coverage of the South, *You Have Seen Their Faces* (1937). But it was as a staff photographer for *Life* and *Fortune* magazines that this remarkably courageous woman gained her widest public audience.

Anxious to promote the human aspect of on-the-scene situations by means of the "mind-guided camera," a term coined by Henry Luce, *Life*'s founder, the photo-magazine's list of contributing photographers is a Who's Who of some of the twentieth century's most gifted image-makers: Alfred Eisenstaedt, W. Eugene Smith, Gordon Parks, Nina Leen, Carl Mydans, and Robert Capa.

ICP: The First Photography Museum

It was the latter's death while photographing in Indochina in 1954 that triggered his brother Cornell Capa's creation of the International Center of Photography (ICP) in New York. The first museum in New York City devoted exclusively to photography, ICP, along with a growing number of other institutions including the Center for Creative Photography in Tucson, Arizona, houses the negatives, personal papers, and prints of many leading photographers. It is a new and forceful indication of the importance now attached to the medium.

Realizing that four other close associates, or "Concerned Photographers" (Werner Bischof, David Seymour, Dan Weiner, and Vytas Valaitis) had also lost their lives while on assignments, Cornell Capa was struck by the fact that the link between photojournalists was their concern

CARLETON WATKINS (1825–1916). *The Vernal Fall,* ca. 1900 (Sotheby Parke Bernet, Inc.).

A San Franciscan, Watkins issued a series of photographs of the West, beginning in 1861. Focused on Yosemite, the Sierra Nevadas, the California redwoods, Watkins' grand views delight collectors as much today as they did 100 years ago.

---

for mankind. "Ours is the first century to be documented by the visual commentary of those who use the camera to express their deeply felt visual convictions," he says.

Altering the approach somewhat to show the effects of the urban environment on people, rather than to show the problems that people face, was another group of photographers, including Bruce Davidson, Lee Friedlander, and Robert Frank. Frank's book *The Americans,* with its introduction by Jack Kerouac, thoroughly shocked viewers when it was published in 1959 because of its brutal insights into shopping centers and six-lane highways. Today, however, it has become a model for countless photographers and publishers who dissect the American landscape.

Among the early British contributors to the "Social Landscape" school, Bill Brandt (1904–   ) and Tony Ray-Jones (1941–1972) were major influences, as well.

Minor White—a Touch of the Mystical

But under the insight of Minor White (1908–1976), distinguished American writer, teacher, and photographer, contemporary photography was also explained as a way to provide viewers an opportunity to dig beneath the surface. Because of its reality, its believability, the medium allows a chance, White felt, to indulge in overtones verging on the mystical. Images can present hidden messages, the onetime editor of the influential magazine *Aperture* said. The work of Aaron Siskind (1903–   ) follows this insight. Concentrating on torn bits of billboard, weathered wood, and graffiti, things that he terms "the detritus of the world," Siskind strives to say more with his camera than his topics will tell at first glance. Harry Callahan (1912–   ), another popular contemporary photographer best known for his delicate images of nature, also looks for messages behind his subjects' masks.

Today, since the decline of the great society and fashion photography era when such currently collectable photographers as Horst, George Hoyningen-Huene, Baron Gayne de Meyer, Steichen, and Cecil Beaton flourished, and the demise of both *Life* and *Look* magazines, and with them the end of the Golden Age of photojournalism, many photographers have now turned to more personal reportage. No longer able to depend on magazines to supply their financial needs, photographers must look to book publishers and collectors, both private and institutional, to fill the void. And it is often museum exhibitions that turn the public's head in a photographer's direction. A show such as the Diane Arbus (1923–1971) exhibit at the Museum of Modern Art in 1972, a record-breaking event that allowed the curious an opportunity to stand and stare at the misshapen and offbeat (freaks, transvestites, nudists) without embarrassment, can help to launch a name in the current Image Race. Publishers and gallery owners now find themselves in the happy situation of having to meet the public's growing demand for acquiring photographs, both to hang on their walls and to look at within the covers of a book.

This lifting of the photographer to a hero status began, many feel, with Michelangelo Antonioni's 1966 film *Blow-Up*. But the "two most fundamental causes of this latter-day revolution are that photography has only recently managed to free itself from the dominance of the other visual traditions and that its message has been borne by an astonishing spread of photographic education," according to Mark Power, head of the photography department at Washington's Corcoran Gallery.* With painters such as Andy Warhol and Robert Rauschenberg emulating photography in the 1960, a movement that has crescendoed with the current Photo-Realism school of painting actually seeking to do with brush, oil, and canvas what photographers achieve with camera, celluloid, and paper, the longtime question "Is Photography Art?" appears to have been answered—at least temporarily!

"I have no interest in persuading people that photography is an art," says John Szarkowski, curator of photography at the Museum of Modern Art, New York City. "It seems to me that we're at least 20 years past that. Now one can proceed to much more interesting questions: What kind of art is it? What are the qualities of it that are special and unique? Who are the photographers exploring what seems to be the most interesting, new, open position?" †

It is a remark whose origins were voiced sixteen years earlier by John Rorimer, then director of the Metropolitan Museum of Art, New York City. "In this era when art enthusiasts are welcoming paintings of white on black and black on white, even white on white, the photographer should have his day in court," Rorimer said.

It was a prophetic remark, one that has come true with a burst of enthusiasm on the gallery and auction house scene. Included among the

* Power, Mark, "Photography: On Its Own," *The Washington Post* (March 15, 1975).

† Jarmusch, Ann, "What Makes a Photograph Great?", *Today, The Philadelphia Inquirer Magazine* (March 14, 1976).

GERTRUDE KASEBIER (1852–1934). *"Blessed Art Thou Among Women,"*
Photogravure, 1900 (Martin Gordon, Ltd.).

Born in Des Moines, Iowa, Käsebier opened a Paris photography studio in
1894. Later in New York, she helped found the Photo-Secession movement.
Enchanted by women and girls, Käsebier was a dyed-in-the-wool romanticist.

expanding number of crowned heads in the current black and white photography kingdom are Danny Lyon, Geoff Winningham, Duane Michals, Emmet Gowin, Grant Mudford, Eva Rubinstein, Les Krims, Judy Dater, Jerry Uelsmann, George Tice, Ralph Gibson, Jack Welpott, Garry Winogrand, and Burk Uzzle. Also there is a growing, but still small, list of currently popular color image-makers as well, including William Eggleston, Stephen Shore, and Neal Slavin.

The Rambunctious School:
Everything Now Acceptable in Photography

Determined to work without preconception or inhibition, many current photographers have gone even further than their forebears to avoid any tampering with their lenses' targets. Nudity taken at the most pubic angles; drug-induced teen-age sex rites; black-leathered motorcycle gangs; all-American used-car lots; burly truck drivers; "anything and everything goes today," says the owner of one of New York's more than thirty galleries showing photographs, up from only one or two ten years ago. Other photographers, members of the "Rambunctious School," delight in writing on their negatives, scratching them, overexposing their film, and double-focusing, plus extensive darkroom manipulation.

But it is the "Conceptual Artists," many of whom work with photographs, yet often refuse to be called photographers, who are the real center-ring performers in the photography circus at the moment. "They may not know their f-stops from their ASA numbers and they may literally black out when they enter a dark room, but they are developing much faster than 'straight' photographers," according to the *Village Voice*'s David Bourdon. "In fact, they are producing the most exciting and innovative photographic work of our time," he believes.*

Practitioners of the new approach include Eleanor Antin, who bought fifty pairs of rubber boots, arranged them in unusual marching configurations on beaches, streets, and pastures—then had her amateur photogra-

* Bourdon, David, "Not Good Ain't Necessarily Bad," *Village Voice* (Dec. 8, 1975), pp. 83–84.

phy friends record them. There's also Bill Beckley. He took photographs of footprints, arranged them on a gallery floor, and led their followers to a photograph of a banana peel.

Is it a put-on? No. Again, according to Bourdon, "most conceptual artists couldn't care less about what constitutes a 'good' photograph. . . . They simply want to put across their ideas as efficiently as possible, and photography seems the most convenient way to do it. . . . They don't get bogged down in technique and are free to let their imaginations soar. . . . Since many of today's artists are 'idea men,' they don't feel obligated to know how to use a camera." *

Sequential images are also popular at this time. An example is Robert Cumming's photo-triptych *The Girl's Story,* in which his subject holds a string between her fingers that (thanks to superimposition in the darkroom) reads, "I like the man a lot." Next she pulls the string taut. Now the message reads, "He liked me more than I like him."

Jan Groover, another creator of sequential images, concentrates mainly on streets and highways, waiting for passing vehicles to alter the image.

The German husband-and-wife team of Bernd and Hilla Becher have also achieved recognition by their straightforward depiction of factories, construction sites, blast furnaces, and the like, but taken from all sides and mounted in grid fashion so that viewers can see 360 degrees around a subject at once.

Other innovative, far-out photographers working in this no-holds-barred vein include Lucas Samaras, Les Krims, Baldessari, Ger Van Elk, Marcia Resnick, and Duane Michals.

Photography No Longer a Minor Art

Putting all the facts together, what does the current excitement about photography mean in terms of the history of the medium? Put simply, photography is no longer a minor art. It is a major art, challenging the traditional art media as never before for space on museum and collectors' walls. One of the reasons for the explosion is that the public—not just

* Bourdon, op. cit.

the students in the classrooms of the world—is turned on to photography as never before. A brief examination of figures shows the force behind the enthusiasm in the United States alone. In 1974, according to the Wolfman Report,* the gross national photo product in the United States in goods and services was $6 billion. Over 90 percent of all Americans have cameras, through the lenses of which roughly seven billion photographs are taken a year, one billion of which are "instant." Will the enthusiasm remain constant? No. It will accelerate. When you consider that, in the next ten years, the twenty-four-to-thirty-four-year-old group, unquestionably the most photographically sophisticated citizens in our society and the most likely new collectors, will increase by 30 percent, or twice the rate of increase of the general public, it stands to reason that the photograph marketplace has barely begun.

"We ain't seen nothing yet," says one dealer who admits to twice the volume of business in 1976 that he experienced in 1975.

Danger Ahead for Photography Collectors

There is inherent danger ahead for the photography collector, though. It is precisely because of the photography *industry's* gargantuan growth that he or she must use extreme good judgment and utmost caution in the selection of images. George Bernard Shaw understood the current situation perfectly when he said that photography was very much like the cod that spawns several thousands of eggs, but brings only one or two to fruition. Not all great photographers have produced consistently great photographs. Nor are all photographers, even though they may have been or are currently being promoted, all that lastingly outstanding. After all, as Edward Weston pointed out, good photographs, like anything else of quality, originate in the creator's brain. Lots of people know how to use a Nikon. Many people know how to use an IBM Executive typewriter, too. But it doesn't necessarily follow that everyone who can look through a lens of a camera and can push a button is creating art, any more than it's logical to assume that anyone who can type is a literary genius.

* Wolfman Report on the Photographic Industry in the United States, 1975–1976 (New York: ABC Leisure Magazines, Inc.).

"Photography—supposedly the most democratic of arts—is, in fact, the most aristocratic," says Douglas Davis. "It mercilessly lays bare dullness or insensitivity because there is no intervening layer of technical engineering, or thick, gooey brush strokes, or carefully modeled clay, to hide behind. At the last, as Stieglitz said, the 'result is the only fair basis for judgment.' " *

The Collector's Challenge

Here is the challenge. It is the ability to separate the images that truly count from the millions that don't. But one thing is sure. Photography is no longer a stepchild of the arts. Whereas it may have once been like those superb medieval brass memorials that line the floors of great English cathedrals and were all too frequently overlooked and stepped on by critics and collectors whose gaze was on "higher things," photography is now the darling of the art world. The achievements of a Stieglitz or a Uelsmann are now seen to be equivalent in importance to those of a Renoir or Warhol.

It cannot be stressed strongly enough, though, that today's new collector must gain a knowledge of the history of the medium if he or she intends to go from the shallow to the deep end of the pool. We've presented only a brief summary of the historic facts. We hope they will inspire a desire to delve more deeply into the fascinating background of the art world's currently awakening giant.

* Davis, Douglas, in *Newsweek* (Oct. 21, 1974), p. 70.

2 | "I Want It; It's Mine"

WHO THE PHOTOGRAPHY COLLECTORS WERE AND ARE

"I indulge my prejudices. That is all I have to say about collecting."
—SAM WAGSTAFF, collector

TO A CHILD, NOTHING IS MORE PRECIOUS THAN HIS BEAT-UP OLD cigar box. Provided, of course, it is full of such treasures as a bluebird's feather; a smooth, white stone; a rubber band, thicker than most, nicer to feel; a dead butterfly, its yellow and black wings outstretched for eternity; and, best of all, a picture of the whole Yankee baseball team.

Collecting is a human instinct, as primitive and basic as reaching up for that first warm, life-sustaining drink of a mother's milk. Possession, or, as psychologists would put it, "possessiveness," is inherent in each of us. Put in economic terms, it boils down to "ownership." The desire to say, "This is mine. I have full rights to it. I can do with it what I want, when I want, and how I want," is there with us all.

For some, it's reduced to simple things. A necklace of shark's teeth around a Polynesian's neck, to symbolize power. For others possession can be more disguised. It can wear the mask of fashion or perhaps of aggressive business. There's the well-dressed housewife who keeps on adding to her already jammed closet. Or the real estate tycoon who can't resist yet another 10,000 acres west of the Pecos.

And most fascinating of all, there's the art connoisseur anxious to hang still more on his overcrowded walls.

45

What is the thread that runs throughout this quest for "things"? Marchel Duchamp answered this question when in 1913 this leading, controversial artist was asked to contribute to an important Paris art exhibit. He found a urinal, signed it, and submitted it. The selection committee panicked. "You can't do that!" they insisted.

"Why not?" Duchamp replied.

"You didn't make it," the committee decreed.

"No. But I *selected* it," Duchamp touchéed, handing over a bicycle wheel and a bottle rack as well.

Artist's Signature and Provenance

In the art field there are two "ingredients" to every work that are of inherent importance to the history of the particular medium as well as to the place within the field of the item itself. First, there's the mark of the creator. It may be as obvious as a genuine signature, or as beneficial as a letter of authenticity from a recognized scholar. (Unknown artists or "attributed to . . ." works can be wonderful, of course. But they are rarely as valuable as universally accepted real McCoys.)

Second, there's the list of who owned the art, those who felt it was important enough to buy it. The "provenance," or this recording of who owned what and when, is a major factor in the value of most established art. Sometimes, of course, it doesn't count—those times when one is gutsy enough to be the first on an ownership list. But more often it's a question of finding out which previous collectors cared enough to say, "Yes, I'll take it. It's mine."

"It's astonishing how rapidly someone can make up their minds about buying a painting when you mention the name of a well-known previous owner," says a reputable Manhattan dealer. "Earlier owners with titles are especially helpful marketing assets."

This pride in one's ownership is as much a driving force today in collecting photographs as it has traditionally been in all the other arts. The number of previous owners of any photograph is minimal, however, compared to those of a Renaissance bronze. The reason is obvious. Photography is a relatively new entry in the art world's vast assortment of publicly acknowledged "collectables." Not that it hasn't been around for close to 150 years. But it is only in the last few years that major publicity has awakened a public response.

Strober Auction Launches Photography into Collecting Consciousness

The Strober auction at PB-84 in New York on February 7, 1970, marked the first truly important entry of photography into the collecting consciousness, according to veteran observers. By commanding respectable prices for the first time, photographs began to be written about, talked about, and fussed over as never before.

The new enthusiasm was sufficiently great that Sotheby Parke-Bernet quickly moved its photo auctions away from less fashionable Eighty-fourth Street and directly into its Madison Avenue headquarters. More recently, leading photography dealer Lee Witkin has installed his new gallery on East Fifty-seventh Street, the center of the art-for-sale world. At the same time, new galleries that sell only photographs are opening throughout the nation and the world, including Boston, Massachusetts; Austin, Texas; Toulouse, France; and Melbourne, Australia. Museums that have never had photographs among their collections have started to do so. Among these are the High Museum in Atlanta, Georgia, and the Art Gallery at the University of Kansas. Corporations have begun to use photographs to decorate their typing pool walls, as well as to bring prestige to their vice-presidents' offices.

And, most revealing of all, some fresh, new private collectors are now on the scene. Recognizing that "the tones created by the action of light on chemicals can be as sensuous and telling as lines etched by hand on copper, it is private collectors, approaching photography as an art medium, who are making the market lively," according to *Fortune* magazine.* These private collectors haven't turned up in droves, however. There are probably far fewer people buying photographs on a continuing

* Mull, Jane, "Investors in the Camera Masterpieces," *Fortune* (June, 1976).

basis than magazines and newspapers would have the public believe, gallery owners confess.

Still, the public interest has been aroused. The remarkable thing about photographs is that the world never had to be persuaded to look at them! Unlike some other artistic media, photography intrigued people immediately upon its inception. Now, though, a growing recognition of photography's ability to stand up tall and be noticed in any artistic lineup has brought it an expanded and growing audience appreciation, especially since the demise of *Life* and *Look*.

"After all, in the long run, they are all images, artistic images, whether a brush or a camera is used," says Sidney Janis, a Manhattan art gallery owner now dealing in photography. "There's a certain feeling in the air as if a new movement has arrived, and somehow the history of the world is beginning to catch up with the contribution of photography." *

For Lee Witkin, the new move toward collecting photographs is the result of revelation. "I think people are discovering there have been major creative people, artists, if you want to say so, working for years, for a century, with the camera. I don't think it's so much photography—that's ridiculous," he says. "People aren't suddenly going to go crazy over watercolor. Watercolor is just a medium. Photography is a medium, too. People are discovering the works of some key artists: Weston, Atget, Siskind." †

Hilton Kramer Forecasts Commercial Boom

Hilton Kramer in *The New York Times* carries this awakening to photography into a forecast for collectors that in the span of three years has already begun to be proved true. "We have only seen the beginning of what promises to be an intellectual as well as commercial boom [in photography]," he wrote. ". . . Contemporary sensibility has become

---

* Janis, Sidney, "The Print Prospectors," *35-MM Photography* (Spring, 1976), p. 68.

† Witkin, Lee, "Photography & Professionals: A Discussion," *Print Collector's Newsletter,* vol. 4, no. 3 (July/August, 1973), p. 54.

EUGENE ATGET (1856–1927). *Shop Window,* Paris, ca. 1910 (Helios Gallery).

Working with the most rudimentary equipment, Atget was one of France's most important early photographers. Yet, he died penniless. Today, Atget's photographs of shop windows, architectural details, and street vendors command top prices.

deeply suspicious of the fictive impulse. It yearns . . . for images that can be tested, if only in theory, by the standards of common experience —and it is increasingly restive, if not resentful, in the presence of the purely imaginary. . . . Photography appears to enjoy a legitimacy denied to the more traditional forms of visual expression. . . . [The fact] that the 'reality' of the photograph itself is often an essay in artifice, a contrivance of timing and technique . . . matters less than the illusion of absolute veracity it is uniquely equipped to convey.

"We do not really expect to see the world the way a great photographer sees it and prints it. Quite the contrary. What we look for in this work is what, out of a lack of opportunity, or deficiency of sensibility, we have missed out on. The photographer functions as a surrogate eye— heightened, alert, tirelessly on the prowl for privileged trophies—and we no more yearn to see the photographer's subjects for ourselves than we yearn for a week-end at Cézanne's Mont Sainte-Victoire. The existence of the photograph is verification enough." *

It boils down to the fact that "photography as a creative medium and a communicative vehicle is no more (or less) diverse, vital, and important than ever," according to A. D. Coleman, another of the still-small but influential circle of photography critics in America today. "Yet the medium's public image is going through a major transition, from bastardy to legitimacy. With legitimacy come certain kinds of attention, prestige, power, and money." †

Because photography is rapidly moving from a minor to a major collectable status, the history of who collected photographs in the past, as well as of those who are collecting today, deserves attention. It is an area still so neglected, however, that the provenance of most photographic images is rarely available. Indeed, one photography dealer seemed astonished that anyone would even query previous ownership when recently asked for such legitimate documentation.

* Kramer, Hilton, "Vision of the Surrogate Eye," *The New York Times* (Dec. 1, 1974).

† Coleman, A. D., "Where's the Money?", *Camera 35,* vol. 19, no. 10 (Jan. 1976), p. 68.

"Anyone familiar with archives knows that there does not exist any object as traditionally neglected, despised, scorned, held in contempt, and consequently destroyed as photographs," says Eugenia Janis, assistant professor of art at Wellesley College. "We know that nothing remains of the work of nearly half the photographers who worked from 1850 to 1860. We have no names even," she says.*

Certainly part of the problem lies in the fact that the entire number of photography historians in the United States is not even equivalent to the number of art historians at one midwestern university. This new field of scholarship is wide open, but fortunately sufficient information does currently exist for new collectors to be able to learn the basics about the history of collecting photographs, as well as about the development of the medium.

Early Photographers Put Together Collections

During the first years after photography was discovered, photographers were often their own collectors. They put together deluxe books, personal albums, and limited-edition portfolios and proudly presented them to friends and institutions. Thought at first to be more of a scientific advance than an artistic one, photography was initially used as an adjunct to words. Libraries were, therefore, especially happy recipients of such works as Peter Henry Emerson's *Life and Landscape on the Norfolk Broads* with its limited number of platinum prints and text by the naturalist Thomas Goodal, as well as William Henry Fox Talbot's *The Pencil of Nature,* in which the photographer pasted his calotypes in by hand. David Octavius Hill and Robert Adamson also presented bodies of their work to museums, while Julia Margaret Cameron recognized her own significance when she proudly distributed her "presentation albums" to illustrious friends.

"Our albums are our salons," wrote Francis Wey in 1851, a statement partly the result of the small size of these early images which, because

---

* Remarks delivered at *Art in America*'s symposium "Collecting the Photograph" (New York, Sept. 20, 1975).

of their delicacy, often needed the security of the pages of a book to preserve them.

The British were especially fond of such photographic preservation, especially of the numerous travel images with which they returned to their homes between 1850 and 1870, and which are eagerly sought after in attics and trunks today.

Others have collected photographs, not because they reflect accepted artistic standards of their day, but because these images often have an inherent historic fascination. Unless the image has been manipulated in the darkroom, the photograph is a true recording of a face, a building, a location, or an event. One early collector, a Frenchman by the name of Gilles, was hypnotized by daguerreotypes because of their accurate recording of what people wore in the nineteenth century. Amassing vast quantities of images that probably would have been destroyed if he hadn't rescued them, Gilles' collection eventually was acquired by the Bibliothèque Nationale in Paris.

Booksellers: Greatest Early Photography Collectors

But of all the early collections, "the greatest accumulations of photographs in the early twentieth century were those of booksellers. This has frequently been overlooked," according to Eugenia Janis.* "The most discriminating private collections of photographs today owe much to booksellers' at times obsessive, and even indiscriminate salvaging and rescuing of photographs destined for the incinerator. . . . Most of the early efforts by booksellers to buy and trade photographs were not successful," she continues, "but their stock eventually was purchased by fastidious collectors who appreciated the fact that photographs from a bookseller were most frequently in complete sets, preserved in their original continuity."

Among these early photographers who added their own powers of discrimination behind a camera to the strength of well-chosen words

* Janis, Eugenia Parry, Introduction, *The Photograph and the Book* (South Woodstock, Conn.: Charles B. Wood, III, Inc., 1976).

PETER HENRY EMERSON (1856–1936). *Cantley: Wherries Waiting for the Turn of the Tide*, from *Life and Landscape on the Norfolk Broads*, 1886 (Helios Gallery).

An advocate of straightforward sharp photography, Emerson delighted in depicting natural scenes: hay-gathering, fishing, duck-shooting, farmers and their families. The simplicity of the French Impressionists greatly influenced Emerson.

---

were Francis Frith, Alvin Langdon Coburn (1882–1966), the Bisson Frères, and Alexander Gardner.

Photographically illustrated books from the middle to the end of the nineteenth century were often expensive, however. A rare and important collection of Timothy O'Sullivan photographs taken from his work on the Wheeler survey in the American West was rediscovered several years ago in Washington's Corcoran Museum. Obviously Corcoran had felt that the book's cost was worthwhile, though, and added it to his vast collection of paintings and sculpture.

The famous Cromer collection, formed in France before World War II, and now at the George Eastman House in Rochester, New York, as well as those put together by André Jammes and Gérard Lévy in Paris, and Helmut and Alison Gernsheim's photography collection, now at the University of Texas in Austin, also deserve capital letters on the list of early pioneers in photography collecting.

America's First Photography Galleries

It was America's Alfred Stieglitz who was to be the United States' most influential spokesman for photography as art in the early twentieth century, however, and whose own work was to be among the most sought after by collectors. Insistent that the medium was competitive with any artistic form, he boldly showed the most avant-garde photographs at both 291 and later An American Place, two of the the country's earliest galleries. He was sufficiently sure of photography, and of himself, in fact, that in 1913 he boldly hung a show of his own works concurrent with the history-making Armory Show.

Stieglitz's influence began to spread and Julian Levy opened a photo gallery in New York to which collectors could turn in the 1930s. There he hung the works of such masters as Cartier-Bresson, Walker Evans, and Atget, charging $25 a print. Unfortunately, nothing sold, and Levy switched to Surrealist painting and succeeded.

New York's Weyhe bookstore on Lexington Avenue offered occasional photographic images to collectors at this time as well. One collector even remembers stumbling over old copies of *Camera Work* here as recently as six years ago. But it was not until 1954, when Helen Ghee opened her Limelight gallery in New York at 91 Seventh Avenue, that the city was to have a truly major new force anxious to promote the work of the world's top photographers. Still, she did not do well. "Sales went very poorly. People weren't as much up to the idea of buying photographs then as they are today," she remembers. "Weston and Cameron prints sold for $75, and the most expensive print I had was a Paul Strand. It was $125. But the average price was $25."

In 1961 Limelight closed. Lack of public interest shut its doors.

A few years later, in the mid-1960s, Robert Schoelkopf provided yet another opportunity for collectors to include photographs among their possessions. Already committed to painting and sculpture as a dealer, he gave Walker Evans a one-man show, and later showed photographs by Brassaï and Cameron.

Carl Siembab in Boston was equally in tune to the upcoming demand for photographs and began his Newbury Street gallery about this same time.

Finally, in 1969, Lee Witkin launched what was to become the first truly successful gallery in New York to concentrate exclusively on photography and to do well. Starting with a $6,000 investment and a $200-a-month rental, Witkin borrowed photographs on consignment from their makers. The time was right and he was quickly on his way. Today it is estimated that the Witkin Gallery grosses over $1 million a year, as does the Lunn Gallery in Washington, D.C., with most of the latter's income from wholesale offerings to other dealers.

Other Manhattan photography galleries that have now become prime sources for collectors include Neikrug, Light, and more recently Marcuse Pfeifer, Helios, and Rinhart. George Rinhart is one of the nation's most influential photography wholesalers, and his 1976 arrival on the retail scene is, in fact, perhaps the most telling piece of evidence of photography's accelerated importance in the eyes of private collectors.

The fall of 1976 also saw the New York opening of both the Images and the K&L color photography galleries, marketing the work of such well-known color craftsmen as Pete Turner, Jay Maisel, and Ernst Haas, as well as Paul Caponigro, George Silk, Eliot Porter, Co Rentmeester, Burt Glinn, and Gordon Parks. Work by these artists, as well as many others currently creating on color film, will become one of the most exciting, collectable aspects of the photography market, it is believed.

Why the Sudden Takeoff for Photography?

But why this major takeoff for photography in the mid-1970s? That is the question which inevitably puzzles many people apprehensive about anything that bubbles to the top so rapidly. After all, they correctly say, it isn't as if the medium was suddenly discovered for the first time. What is it, they ask, that has made the public sit up and take notice at last?

More than any single factor, the skyrocketing prices for paintings and prints in the late 1960s left an enormous void in the art marketplace. With a turndown in the American economy in 1974 and less available discretionary income because of inflation, traditional collectors held back. There was very little affordable for both private and institutional art lovers to focus their budgets on anymore.

Take for an example Patti and Frank K. (Like so many collectors, the couple prefers to remain anonymous.) Sufficiently affluent that they owned graphics by Bellmer, Magritte, Miró, Ernst, Tanguy, and Brauner, they suddenly faced a market where Klee prints started to shoot up in price $5,000 a clip.

"Perhaps the best evidence we can give of the price rises was what happened in 1973 to Picasso's *La Nature morte à la bouteille*," says Frank. "The last recorded price was about $9,000, so when there was a very beautiful impression of it up for sale at the '73 auction, we sent in a bid of $14,000. It sold for $35,000, a price for which we could get a beautiful Picasso drawing. It didn't make sense." *

Harry Lunn presents much the same evidence. Speaking of individual images from Picasso's *Suite Vollard* in contrast to photographs from Gardner's *Photographic Sketch Book of the* [Civil] *War,* he remembers when Vollard prints sold for very little ten years ago, and Gardner's were practically given away. Today, though, he says, "a Vollard plate

* Brody, Jacqueline, "Photography: A Personal Collection," *The Print Collector's Newsletter,* vol. VII, no. 2 (May–June, 1976).

ALFRED STIEGLITZ (1864–1946). *The Flat Iron Building,* Photogravure, 1903 (Graphics International, Ltd./Lunn Gallery).

A recognized master of photography, Stieglitz delighted in capturing New York City landmarks. His image, *The Steerage,* commands over $3,500 in today's rising photo marketplace.

such as plate 27, *Satyr and a Sleeping Woman,* would cost about $10,000, while Gardner's *Harvest of Death* might command $1,200. And, in fact, I'm not sure the Gardner photograph in the history of graphics is any less important than the Picasso. In fact, I would prefer the *Harvest of Death* for my own personal collection."

Realizing that their days of collecting graphics were over, Frank and Patti K, like many others, began to look around for new fields in which to collect. As with a lot of other people, their eyes and their minds focused for the first time on photographs.

"The truth is, photography became a collectable so fast, it's hard to say who pushed the hardest and in what direction," says Jacqueline Brody, editor of *The Print Collector's Newsletter,* one of the first art publications in the United States to cover the medium as part of its regular reportage. "It's been a little bit like spontaneous combustion. No one really lights a match, but suddenly there's fire."

A need by galleries to find inventories of new images able to be sold at reasonable prices was certainly another part of the explanation behind photography's almost overnight push from the wings into center stage. Suddenly dealers woke up to the fact that there had been hundreds of artists producing historically important as well as often visually exciting images, a great many of which were available but had remained out of sight, out of mind. The next logical step was to go out, get them, and offer the photographs for sale to the public.

Purchasing at first a Man Ray and a Moholy-Nagy, Frank and Patti later added works by Paul Strand, Stieglitz, Clarence White, Käsebier, Talbot, and Hill and Adamson. Eventually they were to move into contemporary twentieth-century photography, adding images by Harry Callahan, Emmet Gowin, Benno Friedman, and Robert Cumming. "It would be very easy for me to just like Stieglitz and Strand and Man Ray, but it's always kind of fun if you say, let's see if I can pick up the Man Rays and Stieglitzes of tomorrow," says Frank.

Aware that a contemporary photographer's work priced in the $150 to $300 range costs no more in terms of today's dollar buying power than it did in the 1930s when a Man Ray sold for roughly $40, the couple recognizes that a good deal of today's photography is "no more expensive now than it was when Kertész and Cartier-Bresson were having their first shows in New York. It's really a pretty exciting time. The most innovative and interesting things being done today in the art world are being done in photography."

Nineteenth-Century Photographs Hard to Find

But don't overlook the nineteenth century, warns Arnold Crane, a lawyer and owner of over 55,000 photographs, whose influence and power is among the greatest in the photography market. The proud possessor of the largest private collection of rare photographs in the world, over 2,000 of which are daguerreotypes, including one of Edgar Allan Poe for which he paid somewhere in the $35,000 range, Crane stores his images in a Chicago bank vault.

"There is going to be a dry-up of nineteenth-century material within the next couple of years, from what I understand," he says. "There isn't that much of it, and I feel that the reason dealers are attempting to make such a market in twentieth-century material may well be that they are aware that the nineteenth-century is becoming steadily scarcer and will eventually be unavailable."

Sam Wagstaff, the former curator of contemporary art at the Detroit Institute, is also among the small but passionate group of photo collectors in the United States. Going about his daily photo purchasing with his throttle flat to the floor, he says the reason he collects is "to indulge my prejudices."

Convinced that the years 1973–1975 in photo collecting were equivalent to 1850–1875 in Italy, when the vogue for Italian primitives began and great works of art could be had for little money because they were "primitives," Wagstaff relentlessly prowls galleries, bookstores, antique shops, and photographers' own studios in search of material, a growing amount of which is now contemporary. He is also often asked to speak publicly on his favorite subject.

"It amuses me that an august group such as this would invite someone who has been involved in something for only two years to speak," he told a group of listeners in 1975 at *Art in America*'s "Collecting the

EDWARD S. CURTIS (1868–1952). *A Zuni Woman,* ca. 1900 (Sotheby Parke Bernet, Inc.).

The North American Indian, twenty volumes of text and illustrations by Curtis, is one of the most sought after collector's items. For 30 years, the photographer lived among more than 80 tribes.

Photograph" symposium at Alice Tully Hall in New York. "That wouldn't happen in medicine, or engineering, or any other decent form of endeavor." Going on, he remarked that "I'm convinced that photography is the Esperanto of the art world. We are now at the point where we've been trained by more photographs than any other generation that's lived before us. It's obviously done something to us."

Companies Begin to Buy Photographs

And it's done something to businesses as well, it should be pointed out to new collectors. AT&T, Bell Labs, 3M Company, First International Bank in Dallas: they are among the companies now turning to photography to decorate their walls, often commissioning photographers to produce original images for them.

Judith Selkowitz, a private art consultant hired to put together collections, mainly for large companies, helps to explain the thinking behind these corporations' new ventures. "A lot of companies have full-time art buyers, even art curators, and they come to us. 'We have so much space and so much money,' they'll say. 'Now, do something.' So we begin getting together a collection of etchings, lithographs, wall hangings, and, nowadays, photographs, too. For instance, at the Dime Savings Bank, we included some Berenice Abbotts; at the Andrews Federal Credit Union in Washington, D.C., some George Tices; at Chesebrough Ponds some Brassaïs. Photographs diversify a collection," she says. "To use all the same kind of art is boring. Frequently, in fact, we'll blow up a photograph to cover a certain space. For $2,500 we recently used a photograph to cover an 18-by-5-foot wall in a bank. How else could you do so well for so little?"

The Exchange National Bank in Chicago finds that the six thousand visitors a year who tour its premises to see its vast photography collection merit its art investment. Beginning the corporate acquisitions in 1966 and spending approximately $250,000 so far on some 2,000 prints, bank president William Sax had purchased Edward Steichen's famous portrait of Garbo for $100 when he was only sixteen years old. Continuing to expand the company's collection as well as his own, Sax says that "the art of the second half of the century is photography. People understand it. It moves them." *

Joseph E. Seagram & Sons in New York agrees, realizing that a corporate image is improved by a corporate concern for the arts. Seagram's already extensive contemporary photography collection, put together by the Art Advisory Service offered by the Museum of Modern Art, grew by leaps and bounds in 1976. To celebrate the United States Bicentennial, the company put aside $250,000 and commissioned photographers, including Geoff Winningham, Nicholas Nixon, and Stephen Shore, to record old American courthouses. Soon the collection will tour museums, many of which are freshmen in the ranks of photography collecting.

Museum Collections Increasingly Include Photographs

The New Orleans Museum of Art has moved faster than many of its colleagues, however, in starting an entirely new area of artistic appreciation for its more than one million local citizens. (The Metropolitan Museum of Art, the Museum of Modern Art, the Boston Museum of Fine Arts, the Library of Congress—many of the leading institutions in the nation, as well as London's British Museum, National Portrait Gallery, and the Victoria and Albert Museum, plus Paris's Bibliothèque Nationale and Archives des Documentations Photographiques have been gathering photographs for some years, it should be recognized.) John Bullard, director of the Louisiana museum, jokingly admits that he feels "like a convert to a new fundamentalist sect. I found Photography and was saved." His local constituency is undoubtedly grateful, since about $250,000 has been spent in the last three years by the New Orleans Museum of Art to build up its photography collection.

"We have a $750,000-a-year budget, also about $150,000 to spend a year on new art objects. This isn't a lot of money today," Bullard says.†

---

* Mull, op. cit.

† Remarks delivered at *Art in America*'s symposium "Collecting the Photograph" (New York, Sept. 20, 1975).

"You can hardly buy one truly important painting for this. One of the areas where I figured you do pretty well was photography. . . . I realized that vintage material would go up the fastest in price. Therefore, we delayed to buy contemporary photographers' works for a while."

Concentrating at first on local photographers, primarily on the work of Clarence John Laughlin, a Surrealist as well as an architectural image-maker, later including works by Sander, F. H. Evans, Doisneau, Weston, and Cunningham, the museum continues to look for images of photogra-

---

KARL BLOSSFELDT (1865–1932). *Dipsacus laciniatus, #3,* ca. 1920 from a portfolio of 12 prints, edition of 50 (Sonnabend Gallery).

A professor at the Berlin Academy of Art and Design, Blossfeldt's avocations were photography and botany. Architects, he believed, should look to nature for inspiration.

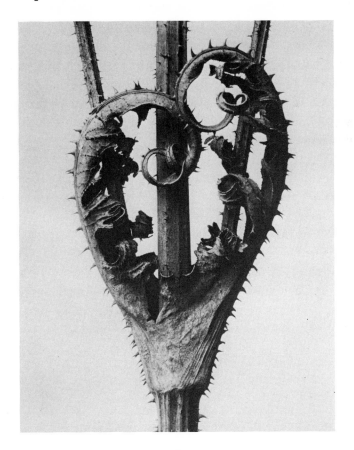

phers who worked in New Orleans, among them E. J. Bellocq and Arnold Genthe.

"One day I was showing a possible acquisition to our Board of Trustees. It was Genthe's photograph of an elderly black woman, 'The Faithful Servant,'" Bullard recalls. "Suddenly, one of the trustees looked startled and broke into the conversation. 'Why, that's a photograph of our old washer woman, Maude,' he said. And it was. This person even remembered the day Genthe had taken Maude's picture. The wonder of photography is that a good deal of its history is still a part of our own lifetime." *

Avedon Show at Marlborough Gallery— a Turning Point

Many veteran observers of the photography scene feel that the most historic event on the recent collecting front has been the entrance of the large, big-name galleries into the marketplace. Marlborough Gallery, with its 1975 exhibition of fashion photographer Richard Avedon's photographs, was clearly the first to make the headlines. With the photographer's candid portraits of famous people, often looking their worst, and frequently blown up to mural size, the three-week show drew up to three thousand people a day, and sold over $12,000 worth of catalogs, to say nothing of the volume of photographs that moved off Marlborough's walls into new owners' hands.

Stating that "I must be held responsible for what you are seeing here. . . . I can't blame the images on a magazine editor, or bad reproduction. You're seeing the original print. I'm naked," † Avedon priced the photographs for between $175 and $20,000.

It is precisely this upward trend in photography prices—particularly for nineteenth-century and early-twentieth-century "vintage" photographs, usually higher priced than works of most living photographers—that has attracted the most famous art galleries, both European and American,

* Bullard, op. cit.

† *Time* (Sept. 22, 1975), p. 71.

ARNOLD GENTHE (1869–1942). *Carmel Snow* (Sotheby Parke Bernet, Inc.).
Cool, crisp, controlled: the qualities of this sophisticated portrait of Carmel
Snow, editor of *Harper's Bazaar*, reflect the elegance of its subject and the classic
simplicity of the photographer. Photographs of "known" people inevitably
fetch higher prices than those of the "unknown."

to selling photographs. "When important photographers' works, historic ones in particular, were only selling for peanuts, it didn't warrant our getting into the market," a leading gallery owner admits. "We couldn't make enough profit on sales to merit the bookkeeping involved. Now, when prices are rising, it has begun to be profitable to sell photographs. And our gamble is that it will become even more so."

In certain cases, this new development has produced antagonism. A. D. Coleman voiced it when he wrote of "the long-suppressed sense of outrage and injustice the photographic community feels toward the art establishment, which has ignored photography for so many years and is now sniffing around the medium only because there's something to be had from it." *

And Robert Schoelkopf comes right out and says that "the big boys now see that photography may be worth money to them. They weren't interested when Walker Evans was selling for $100, that's for sure, but they are interested when Walker Evans is selling for $1,000." †

Included among these "interested" galleries are Castelli Graphics in New York, as well as Sonnabend and Zabriskie, both with Manhattan and Paris addresses. They are among the pace-setters today in promoting and marketing photography.

Photographers Give Negatives to Center for Creative Photography

On the curatorial and research side, the Center for Creative Photography (CCP) at the University of Arizona in Tucson has given a new dimension to photography collecting as well. The repository of the negatives and correspondence of five of America's most important living artists— Ansel Adams, Wynn Bullock, Frederick Sommer, Harry Callahan, and Aaron Siskind—the center's existence and extensive funding testifies to

* Coleman, A. D., "Where's the Money?", *Camera 35,* vol. 19, no. 10 (Jan., 1976), p. 29.

† Deschin, Jacob, "The Print Prospectors," *35-MM Photography* (Spring, 1976), p. 116.

the new appreciation and honor that photographers are beginning to experience. Including, it should be mentioned, those who practice snap-shooting, both professionals and amateurs. "Anthropologists and sociologists share the feeling that the common snapshot presents the most accurate reflection of our society since the invention of the hand-held camera," a center spokesman says. "It is felt that they are not so much 'naïve' photographs, but important artifacts."

It is true that there is currently an entire snapshooting school of photography that has found a sympathetic response on the part of several leading galleries and museums. However, the majority of private photography collectors continue to be more conservative. The tried-and-true images have the greatest selling appeal.

Collectors' Insistence on "Well-Known" Images

And herein lies one of the photography market's greatest problems and challenges. It is a universally accepted fact that new collectors, as well as many of the established ones, want only the well-known images—those photographs which have appeared frequently in books or on museum walls. "I have had bad dreams where I have traveled through museum after museum in America, past the Henry Moores, through the courts into the lovely Pei, Kahn, or Johnson interiors, into the elegantly appointed photography galleries where I have seen 'Moonrise, Hernandez' by Mr. Adams, 'Picnic on the Bank of the Marne' by Cartier-Bresson, 'Canyon de Chelly' by Timothy O'Sullivan, any portrait of Tennyson by Mrs. Cameron, 'Pepper 30' by Evans, etc. etc. until all the golden Weston chestnuts were exhausted. I don't think that's the most exciting way to go," says John Szarkowski, director of the department of photography at New York's Museum of Modern Art. "Curators who defend what they buy or hang on the grounds that 'it's being done' should be hung by their thumbs 'til they give a more responsive answer," he feels.*

It is this "collecting by the book" that has many gallery owners and

* Remarks given at *Art in America*'s symposium "Collecting the Photograph" (New York, Sept. 20, 1975).

LEWIS HINE (1874–1940). *Little Orphan Annie,* 1909 (Collection of the Library of Congress).

In the early twentieth century, children were often forced to work at dangerous jobs in factories, ten to twelve hours a day. Hine was horrified. His photographs were instrumental in promoting passage of child labor laws.

---

photographers the most disturbed today. For the artist, it's a question of "having to print and reprint the same images again and again," according to Jerry Uelsmann, "of not having sufficient time to go out to produce new ones, you're so busy in the darkroom with the old ones."

For the gallery owner, it's the problem of being less successful selling generally unknown images by a photographer. To remedy this situation, New York's Light Gallery recently raised its prices on the tried-and-true images in the hope of shifting customers' eyes in the direction of as yet

AUGUST SANDER (1876–1964). *Circus People,* 1930 (Collection of the Museum of Modern Art).

One of Germany's finest photographers, Sander captured his subjects as they really were, and not as they wished the world to see them. He is said to be a major influence on the work of Diane Arbus.

---

unknown photographs by the same artists. "As these lesser-known images begin to become more popular and the photographer has to start printing a lot of them, then we'll raise the price," says director Victor Schrager. "What we hope this new approach will do is to free the photographer from returning to the same negative all the time. And to attract collectors to images that may start to appreciate more rapidly in value."

Harry Lunn also laments the current lack of collector imagination and daring. "A colleague of mine described his reaction to an exhibition of recent photographic acquisitions several years ago in a major museum," he says. "There was something hauntingly reminiscent about it and suddenly he realized why. Each and every image was one that had been illustrated in Newhall's *History of Photography.* This same lack of imagination is characteristic of many private collectors. The Stieglitz print must be *The Steerage,* the Paul Strand must be the image of the white fence, and so on. This isn't to take away any of the importance of these exceptional images. But, after all, Stieglitz and Strand took many interesting photographs and it is sometimes of interest to include a work that is less an obvious signature of the artist."

To those beginning to collect photographs the field is enormous. Unlike the situation in print, painting, and sculpture, where most of the truly great masterpieces have been snatched up and are off the market forever, great masterpieces by photographers, both from the past as well as those currently still producing, are to be found. At higher prices than five or even two years ago, of course, but at prices that nevertheless continue to be remarkably reasonable.

Peter Bunnell, director of the Princeton University Art Museum, is one of the most optimistic judges of photography's continued rise in prices. At the same time, he is straight to the point when he defines what makes any art collection stand out as great. "No one has been remembered for the collection that has been amassed," he says. "The ones that are remembered are the ones that are selected." *

Marcel Duchamp understood this fact sixty-four years ago with his urinal, his bicycle wheel, and his bottle rack. People are still talking about his selection.

Once one accepts that astute selection is the primary ingredient in forming any collection of art, the next step is to know how and when to begin.

* Bunnell, Peter, "News of the Print World: People & Places," *The Print Collector's Newsletter* (New York, Nov./Dec., 1975).

3 | "Look, Look, Look"

HOW TO PREPARE TO FACE THE PHOTOGRAPHY MARKET AND KNOW WHAT TO COLLECT

"Photographers publish too much too soon, and their bad photos spoil their good ones. Time makes a selection for you. The nice thing about having lived as long as I have is that you can see much more clearly what is good—which photos you can show and which ones you do better to throw away."

—BRASSAÏ

IN ANY CREATIVE AND ATHLETIC ENDEAVOR, THERE IS ONLY ONE way to improve. Practice. The same rule holds true for art collectors, too, according to museum curators and gallery owners. "It's a combination of mental perception and physical endurance," one energetic collector says. "You have to go out and look, look, look. Sometimes at the end of a day's gallery-hopping, my feet hurt as badly as they did when I sold housewares at Macy's one college vacation. But all the looking in the world isn't going to do you any good if you haven't any idea of what to look *for,* or what you are looking *at* once you're standing in front of it."

So where do you begin?

"You immerse yourself in books of photographs," counsels Weston Naef, assistant curator of prints and photographs at New York's Metropolitan Museum of Art. "Before anyone buys his first print, he must know what the world of editors, publishers, scholars, and critics have defined as 'desirable pictures.' Considering that photography is an exceedingly ubiquitous medium with literally millions of pictures having been made and still being made each day, the key question becomes, 'How do I sort out from these millions of photographs those worth preserving?' Not every photograph has intrinsic value. Only certain ones do."

EDWARD JEAN STEICHEN (1879–1973). *Stieglitz and his Daughter,* platinum print, 1905 (Collection of the Metropolitan Museum of Art).

Considered "the dean of American photographers," Steichen was the best-known photographer of his day. His works are currently among the most expensive. A Steichen print, *Nocturne,* Versailles, 1910, sold in 1976 for $4,750.

Proliferation of Books of Photographs

Fortunately, in the last couple of years publishers have begun to produce more books of photography, both by the world's most famous photographers and by newcomers. It was only a short while ago, however, that collectors would have had an extremely hard time learning to train their eyes through the effective utilization of books. Publishers were slow to catch up with the public's enthusiasm for owning reproductions of these works in both hard and soft cover. Now, though, one can sit down with titles ranging from *André Kertész: Sixty Years of Photography: 1912–1972* to Danny Lyon's *Conversations with the Dead,* a body of photographs dealing with prison life; from Judy Dater and Jack Welpott's amply natural *Women and Other Visions* to Brassaï, *The Secret Paris of the 30's,* a revelation of the French capital's morals of the time.

With many of the photo books collectable themselves, especially those now out of print, their initial purpose for a viewer is to make him ask, "Which photographs do I like? Which photographs don't I like?" These are the two easiest questions to wrestle with, Naef believes. "But it is the in-between images, those which trigger no response at all, which really deserve the inquisitive collector's attention," he says.

The fact is, they, too, have been selected for the book by the photographer and the editor. One must therefore assume they were thought worth publishing. If one doesn't agree with the choice, then one must define why. The more mental grappling of this sort one does, the more defined one's sense of aesthetics will become.

"The collector still may not like the photographs, but if he has been able to articulate *why* not, then he's moving ahead," Naef says.

Reading such basic texts as Beaumont Newhall's *The History of Photography* as well as Helmut and Alison Gernsheim's *A Concise History of Photography* (neither of which mentions some of the most talked-about photographers today) is, of course, indispensable in establishing the foundation for any collector's own scholarship. But also consider such opportunities as attending the lectures given by many museums on photography's role in the art world. They, too, serve as an extremely worthwhile route for newcomers to the photography-collecting field who want to familiarize themselves with key practitioners and their work. Adult education courses, symposiums financed by foundations and publications, summer photography workshops given at universities and by groups of photographers themselves: these also provide a way for collectors to learn a good deal about the background of the medium and to hone their own tastes.

Consider a Darkroom Course

"But there is nothing better than getting your hands wet in the chemicals themselves, learning the actual technicalities of the medium, the darkroom side of things, too," says Casey Allen, moderator of the television program *In & Out of Focus.*

"You will never know what a truly fine photography print is unless you know what is required to make one," he says. "Only then can you, as a collector, judge the fine print skills of a photographer who is a masterful darkroom technician versus the mediocre print of a photographer who is not. Or who doesn't care."

Since, as Ansel Adams says, "the negative is the score, the print is the performance," such personal familiarity with the printing process itself cannot help but allow a collector a greater sense of security and confidence when making a purchase.

Getting to meet and hopefully to know some of the collectable photographers themselves adds still greater dimension to an aspiring collector's own judgment. Again, leading schools frequently offer lecture series where such people as Inge Morath, Arnold Newman, Bobbi Carey, Eddie Adams, Arthur Tress, George Tice, and Anna-Lou Liebovitz are willing to conduct a dialogue with an audience.

The International Center of Photography in New York has, in fact, built up an annual attendance of approximately 3,000 interested listeners to its array of famous photographers in the last three years.

By hearing these people speak and learning from them exactly what they must go through in order to take a photograph, a much greater sympathy as well as a more refined vision by the collector himself can

---

IMOGEN CUNNINGHAM (1883–1976). *Leaf Pattern,* before 1929 (the Imogen Cunningham Trust).

A sassy, little lady, still an active photographer when she died in 1976 at the age of 93, Cunningham had been a member of the California f/64 group, dedicated to clean, simple art form.

result. Personal taste will be drawn toward certain photographers' images. Also, newcomers will come to grips with the issue of whether they want to collect contemporary photographs, works by people living today and in their prime, or whether they wish to delve into the past and have a collection that is more historic, that contains more undisputed big names.

Whether one is interested in photographs purely as an investment will play a part here, of course. If so, vintage images will be one's primary focus of attention. If potential financial rewards aren't of paramount importance, then the work of young artists can attract more study and acquisition. However, "steady nerves and a strong conviction of the rightness of one's own judgment are needed to collect in the avant-garde area," critic Gene Thornton warns. "For no one can ever be certain what part of today's avant-garde will be tomorrow's classic. However, the rewards could be a pace-setting collection that could grow in value and esteem." *

Proliferation of Photo Galleries

At this point, the actual purchasing process can begin. "After dog-paddling for so long, you eventually have to learn how to stroke out," a collector says. "You have to put theory into practice." Clearly the most conspicuous source of photographic images now are the galleries, both in large cities and in small towns, both in the United States and abroad. Multiplying faster than the yellow pages of the telephone book can list them, they are more in evidence in New York City than anywhere else. At least thirty photography and private photography dealers, many of whom sell paintings and graphics, too, now offer collectors inventories to go through in Manhattan. Most are open Tuesdays through Saturdays, and only a few of the private dealers require advance appointments.

The level of sophistication varies enormously, though. Well-established galleries in prime urban areas inevitably have a Bigelow on the floor, a Weston to the front of you, an Adams to the rear, Imogen Cunningham

---

* Thornton, Gene, "The Zooming Market for Photographic Prints," *Town & Country* (March, 1975), p. 49.

on the right, Berenice Abbott on the left. Less affluent galleries, frequently run by photographers themselves, perhaps even a camera club, settle for hardwood floors, exposed plumbing, low rent, and very often some of the most progressive work by newcomers in the field today.

A look at the list of galleries in leading photography magazines, Sunday art sections of newspapers, and in the back of this book will present the collector with sufficient addresses to keep him busy on a regular round of sleuthing out pictures.

Confidence in Dealer Important

It is extremely important to find a dealer in whom you can have confidence. That is usually determined by his track record—who he represents; who his other customers are; who he has "discovered." Normally, it is also wise to deal with someone who has been in business at least five years. Of course, this is difficult with photography collecting so new. But the point is that a collector wants to be sure a dealer will be around in the future if he has to lodge a complaint. Most important of all, though, he must have rapport with a dealer if he intends to do business with him regularly. A dealer must be able to understand exactly what a collector is looking for to help him build up his collection. And when a dealer advises a collector, the collector must feel that the dealer's taste and judgment is astute.

In short, as with any interpersonal relationship, a collector and dealer who work regularly together establish a mental atmosphere, which should be conducive to growth and satisfaction for the purchaser. After all, it is his wallet that is being thinned.

"There is nothing more important for a collector than determining which dealers he feels the most comfortable with, those who will treat him the fairest and squarest," confirms a couple who spent several years "shopping around" until they settled on two galleries with which they deal regularly today. "If a gallery owner likes you, he will frequently alert you to a particular photograph's availability way before he puts it on his walls. If he sees that you are trying very hard to refine and build up your collection, he'll go out of his way to help you.

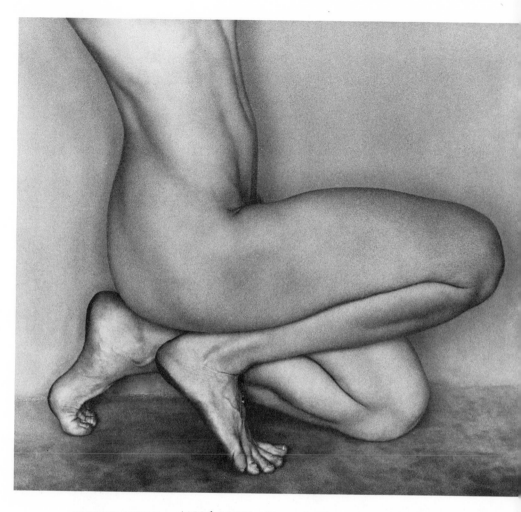

EDWARD WESTON (1886–1958). *Dancer's Knees,* 1927 (Collection of Cole Weston).

Due to limited finances at the beginning of his career, Weston seldom used more than two sheets of paper to make a print. Consequently, he became one of the finest darkroom technicians.

"Sure, dealers are in business to make money. But, for the most part, they really like what they're selling. It stands to reason that they'll be the most favorably inclined to customers who share this same enthusiasm."

One of the mistakes that many newcomers to photography make is that they "walk into a gallery for the first time, look at what's on the wall, then walk out. They think they've seen everything," says Leslie Simitch of Enjay Gallery in Boston. "But it isn't so."

Drawers of photographers' work are usually available to anyone who asks to see them in a gallery.

"One new collector, Bing Wright from Seattle, came in and went through absolutely every single image we had in stock. It took him four days. Finally he made up his mind and bought quite a few photographs," says Victor Schrager, director of New York's Light Gallery. "The remarkable thing was, Bing was only seventeen years old at the time. It's amazing how young some collectors now are!"

Another reason that gallery-going is important is that a photographer's works that haven't been seen anywhere else may turn up unexpectedly. Grant Mudford is an example. Walking into a Madison Avenue gallery one day, shortly after he arrived in the United States from Australia, he opened his portfolio and showed the owner his black and white insights into galvanized steel fences, moving vans, and office buildings. The result was an exhibition almost immediately and steady sales ever since. "We liked his work and were willing to take a chance," the gallery director says. "But, I admit, we didn't think the public would react so favorably so quickly."

Auctions a Major Source of Photographs

Auctions have also become prime sources of photographs for today's collector. Christie's and Sotheby's in London, Martin Gordon, Inc., and Sotheby Parke Bernet Inc. in New York: these are some of the leading exchanges where buyers and sellers who are willing to hold their breath can hope for the best. With catalogs available through the mail, interested out-of-town collectors can make their selections by studying the printed photographs and can then send in their bids.

"It is always better to be there in person, though," cautions an experienced auction-goer, "and to have seen the images at the exhibition beforehand. Your choice may not look as good 'in the flesh' as it did in catalog reproduction. And a mail-order bid can lose out by $25 or $50 to someone who's in the room at the time of the actual auction."

"Something rather ironic about photographs in catalogs is that people frequently say, 'Oh! It looked better on the page than it does now that I see the real thing,'" says Anne Horton of Sotheby Parke Bernet Inc. "What has happened is that people are now so used to printing's half tones that pure black and white throws them."

Different Types of Photographs Are Collectable

Used bookstores, flea markets, antique shops, anywhere that graphics are sold will also usually include photographs. Unlike a few years ago, though, they will probably be recognized for their worth by their owners. Unless, of course, you find them in a family trunk. Here you may discover some of the most collectable items currently catching people's attention. These include:

1. *Postcards.* Brightly colored old postcards are especially popular. They are frequently of such natural landmarks as Niagara Falls and the Grand Canyon. Sam Wagstaff began collecting this way. "I even go through the postcard racks today at airports when I travel," he says. "It's amazing what you can find. Postcards relate to common taste, and in many ways, that's what photography is all about."

2. *Stereographs.* A source of an evening's entertainment in many American and European homes at the turn of the century, these double images are often buried beneath great-grandmother's wedding dress. Those that have come out of hiding are rising in price and are being sought with increased stamina by collectors. "I think [stereo views] are the greatest thing in photography, telling more effectively the history and sociology of the world than any other photographic medium," says George Rinhart. "As a businessman, I see the stereo field as the biggest thing in photography today."

Fortunately, thousands of these cards remain. In 1858, for instance,

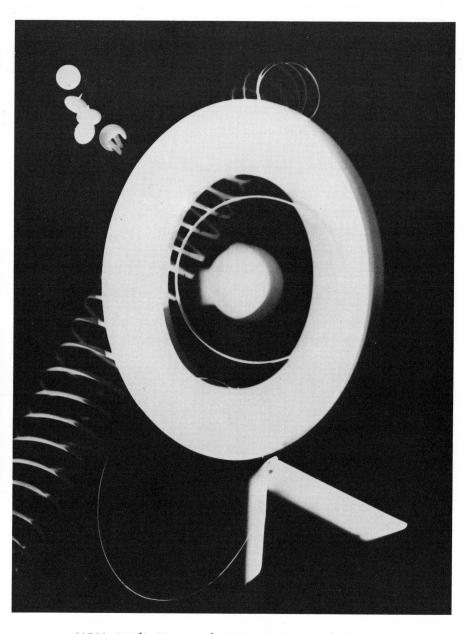

MAN RAY (1890–1976). *Rayograph,* 1922 (Collection of Timothy Baum).
    Like many of his colleagues, Man Ray had been a painter before turning to
the photographic medium. His well-known "rayographs" were made by placing
objects on photographic paper and exposing them to light. Because there is no
negative in this process, the images are one of a kind.

the London Stereoscopic Company advertised over 100,000 different photographs for sale, usually of architectural and topographic subjects. A year later, the Stoddard Company in New York boasted an equal number of images available, many of western scenes by photographers recognized today for their superior skills.

3. *Daguerreotypes.* One of the earliest forms of photography, daguerreotypes were images on copper plates. Since Daguerre wasn't able to

---

PAUL STRAND (1890–1976). *Automobile Wheel,* N.Y., 1917 (Light Gallery).

Strand's position on straight photography and the strength of his contribution to the medium is expressed in his statement: "The full potential power of every medium depends upon the purity of its use, and all attempts at mixture end in such dead things as the colour etching, the photographic painting and, in photography, the gum print, etc., in which the introduction of handwork and manipulation is merely the expression of an impotent desire to paint. . . ."

master the duplicating process, each daguerreotype is unique. The result is a true collector's item, with prices steadily inching higher all the time. Still, the word hasn't permeated the entire countryside yet. An auction in rural Virginia netted one collector two dozen daguerreotypes for $18 last spring—a real giveaway by New York standards.

4. *Tintypes, or ferrotypes.* Tintypes were mostly of people, as were daguerreotypes. Taken on lacquered iron rather than on copper plates, they were less expensive. Snubbed by collectors for a while, tintypes are now coming into their own.

5. *Cartes-de-visite.* Small in size, meant to replace calling cards, cartes sold by the hundreds of millions in the 1860s and 1870s in America and in Europe. Usually portraits of people, including royalty, politicians, writers, society, music-hall stars, courtesans, they are normally about 2¼ x 3½ inches, sepia-toned, mounted on cards, and often with the photographer's name and address on the reverse side or beneath the picture. Frequently the name of the sitter is engraved, as well. The fashion for collecting cartes in albums, like stamps, also extended to rarer images, including animals and architecture.

Other vintage photographic images that are becoming more popular with collectors are those dealing with topography, a term defined by the dictionary as "the detailed mapping or charting of the features of a relatively small area, district, or locality." In short, travel photography, but usually of a hundred years ago. The Bisson Frères, Louis Auguste and Auguste Rosalie, excelled in this school in the 1860s, when they were part of the Empress Eugénie's entourage. Visiting Switzerland with the court, the Bisson brothers took some of the most striking Alpine photographs in the history of the medium. Later, they indulged their love for beauty with images of French and Italian churches and cathedrals.

A 1976 exhibition at Asia House in New York City of photographs taken in India by British and native photographers during the second half of the nineteenth century has now awakened collectors to this nation's photographs. An extraordinary exhibition the same year of photographs taken in Brazil from 1840 to 1920 turned New Yorkers' heads south of the border, too. Totally unknown outside of Brazil until their appearance at the Center for Inter-American Relations on Park Avenue, the pictures are "of equivalent quality and variety to the work being done during the same period anywhere else in the world," according to Weston Naef, guest curator of the show.

Fashion and Hollywood Photographs Increasingly Popular

Other fields of photography demanding more attention recently are those of fashion—triggered by a recent exhibition entitled "Fashion Photography: Six Decades" at Hofstra University—and of pre–World War II Hollywood. A show at M. Knoedler and Co., Inc. in New York in April, 1976, that included Cecil Beaton's full-length portraits of Gary Cooper and Tallulah Bankhead, Eisenstaedt's Will Rogers, and Horst's Joan Crawford helped fan the desire of collectors for these nostalgic, beautifully composed early prints. At the same time, early fashion photographs by Baron de Meyer, Steichen, Peter Rose Pulham, Louise Dahl Wolfe, Hoyningen-Huene, and again Horst, are all emerging from their false labels of commercial photography into the bright light of art and therefore becoming collectable.

In fact, it is this later development, beginning seriously about 1975, that is anticipated to be one of the most exciting aspects of future photography collecting. Though commercial photographers were long neglected by dealers and collectors because they earn their living shooting photographs for advertising and editorial use (a "taboo" in the eyes of many who believe steady income takes away from the "art for art's sake" integrity of a medium), their work is now being looked at anew. It should be remembered, however, that Edward Steichen worked for the J. Walter Thompson Advertising Co., a fact frequently swept under the rug. His compositions for Jergen's Lotion and for Kodak were proclaimed as milestones at the time.

Commercial Photographers Sought After by Collectors

While the work of such masters as Irving Penn, who has included advertising work in his repertoire, can now be purchased through a gallery, it is still true that, more often than not, collectors must seek out so-called commercial photographers' works directly from their creators. "I have had requests for years from the public for my work," says Pete Turner. "And, I confess, I haven't paid much attention to them. Now, though, with the spotlight turned more in our direction, even more collectors are asking me to print them an image. I can see that I will have to do something about it . . . soon."

Hiro, a Richard Avedon pupil, is another artist whose genius behind a camera is sought after, but whose prints are hard to obtain. "We can see that the time is fast approaching when Hiro will have to face the question of being 'collectable' and therefore make some of his images available to the marketplace," an assistant in the photographer's studio tells callers.

Deborah Turbeville, a former editor on *Mademoiselle* magazine and now a photographer whose dreamlike scenes are bathed in hazy, impressionistic tonalities, is already cashing in on the demand by collectors for fashion's outré look. Printing limited-edition black and white images at $400 and up, Turbeville's creations are described by *Newsweek* as "choreographed like a ballet. . . . They look like scenes out of Bertolucci or Antonioni's alienated 'The Red Desert.' Her people are glued to their environment in a mood of overwhelming dreamlike silence." *

Then there is Helmut Newton, a star of French *Vogue,* who "sees women as gorgeous animals—with the emphasis on the animal. His erotic photos are often lush and decadent, implying danger and recalling Berlin of the '30s." †

In his book *White Women* Newton shocks by showing models in couturier clothes who delight in protruding one breast, crack whips, and strike erotic poses in black garter belts and boots, inevitably with flagrant overtures of lesbianism. "I have always been interested in the sexual side," Newton says. "If people think my photos are erotic or disgusting, thank God they're touched by them." ‡

* "Fashion's Kinky Look," *Newsweek* (Oct. 4, 1976), p. 99.

† Op. cit.

‡ Op. cit.

DOROTHEA LANGE (1895–1965). *Spring Plowing in a Cauliflower Field,* 1937 (Collection of the Library of Congress).

Lange was one of the "Compassionate Photographers" who worked for the Farm Security Administration in the early 1930s. These FSA photographers recorded the conditions of Midwestern farmers during a four-year drought and the effects of sophisticated farming operations on the small family farm.

Bourdin and the New Eroticism

There is also Guy Bourdin, clearly one of the most daring fashion photographers in Paris, who brought his subcult creativity to Manhattan's Bloomingdale's department store. Tapping the unknown to become the known, he singled out six girls from off Lexington Avenue, posed them in various stages of lacy undress to launch the store's new lingerie boutique through the pages of a color catalog, and started still another rush in the process. Bourdin's photographs, one with an unmistakably erect, baby-blue penis floating in midair, are "ambiguous vignettes, suggestive of 'je ne sais quoi'—smoldering-satin-eroticism, triple bedded double entendres, Stepford wifery, Bergman heavy breathing, and Story of O-isms," according to *New York* magazine. The result? For Bloomingdale's, the creation of a promotion piece that has all the potential of becoming an important historic document, worthy of collecting!

Not everyone shares the current enthusiasm for this field of kinky fashion photography, however. "Bourdin is one of my favorite photographers," says Duane Michals, whose dream photographs are among the most collectable images on the market. "And I love fashion photography. I shoot a lot of it myself. But I don't consider fashion photographs as 'art.' They're interesting sociologically, historically, but they are exactly what they depict. They reflect what is in vogue at the moment they were shot. They don't, therefore, have the mark of infinity. They aren't what the photographer *wants* to photograph. They are what he's been paid to shoot. If a collector is willing to accept these parameters, fine. But he should be aware that, like so much in life, a great deal depends on the definitions."

Consider, for instance, press photography. Is it collectable? Some people think so, including Cecil Beaton and Gail Buckland, authors of *The Magic Image.* "The public is apt to take for granted the excellence of the photographs seen every day in the newspapers," they say. "It does not realize the expertise needed to capture the publishable picture: It does not realize that most probably it was taken under conditions of extreme difficulty, possibly even danger." * Such famous photographs as the three English Queens (Mary, Elizabeth, and Elizabeth II) swathed in black at the funeral of King George VI and Nick Ut's world-shattering *Vietnamese Children Fleeing from Fire Bomb* have registered indelibly in the minds of millions of viewers, however.

* Beaton, Cecil and Buckland, Gail, *The Magic Image* (Boston/Toronto: Little, Brown & Co., 1975), p. 286.

Weegee: Press Photographer Par Excellence

And so have many of the photographs by New York's Arthur H. Fellig (1899–1969), better known as "Weegee." Working as a printer in a news-picture agency at the start of his career in order to afford film that he shot on his own time at night, the cigar-chewing, raucous, vainglorious Polish immigrant stamped "Credit Weegee the Famous" on the back of his photographs. Perhaps rightly so! With a short-wave set by his bed, in which he slept with his clothes on, he was alerted to the city's disasters and able to record them on film, frequently before the police arrived. Fires, crimes, accidents: they all intrigued Weegee. But the humorous did, too. One of his best-known photographs was taken in a bar with a tuxedoed drunk stroking the pig of a farmer sitting nearby.

"A problem which early photojournalists faced was that their negatives were owned by their employers," says Cusie Pfeifer, owner of Marcuse Pfeifer Gallery in Manhattan. For instance, many photographs by Margaret Bourke-White were taken when she was on the staff of *Fortune* and *Life;* their sale through a gallery produces revenue for Time-Life as well as the gallery itself. "It never occurred to the photographer or his employer in many cases that these people's work would eventually be thought of as collectable. Nowadays, however, a photojournalist, or any photographer hired to do special assignments for publishers or companies, tries to make sure that his contract reads that he maintains the rights to his work."

All photographers, in fact, now recognize there is a larger market for their work than was ever before thought possible. Still, in many cases, collectors find it time-consuming to track down the photographers whose work they see in public media and would like to buy. Howard Daitz, a private dealer, has been one of those willing to do so. "I would see a reproduction in a magazine that I liked and would take as much as six months to track down the photographer. I would write him for a print and then maybe a year later I would get it," he says.

Dance photography—including the work of pioneer Barbara Morgan (1900–   ), who spent five years interpreting the movements of Martha Graham; Hoppé's studies of the Diaghilev ballet corps; and Avedon's

ANDRÉ KERTESZ (1894–   ). *Martinique, 1972* (Light Gallery).
The infinite aesthetics seen in Kertesz's body of work indicate a flexible and probing eye. The average photographer, standing on the balcony of a tourist hotel, might not have seen this graphic, transcendental image.

_____

strobe shots of Rudolf Nureyev—also fascinates certain collectors. As do unusual photographs, both old and new, printed on such materials as cloth, leather, enamel, porcelain, and artificial ivory. Or historic photographs of one subject only, for instance: the construction of the Empire State Building; life in Harlem in the 1920s and 1930s; antique motorcars; suffragettes; the laying of the tracks of the Transcontinental Railroad.

LAZLO MOHOLY-NAGY (1895–1946). *Halt!* Fotoplastik, ca. 1925 (Graphics International, Ltd./Lunn Gallery).

Moholy-Nagy, an early worker in photography, became dissatisfied with the medium's strictly reproductive nature. He therefore began to use photography in a more creative way. For example, he photographed his collages, or Fotoplastiks, as he called these images.

There is really nothing sacred, nothing that should be out of a collector's interest range. As the world delves more deeply into the history of photography, new areas in which photographers have concentrated will open up, to be of increased interest to collectors. Just as the camera is able to record infinite subjects, so will collectors be faced with infinite choices to make.

Specialization—Key to Future Photo Collecting

Specialization, therefore, will be the name of the game in future photography collecting, dealers and many collectors themselves forecast. With rising prices for historic prints, broad-based collections with first-quality images from 1839 up to the present will be harder to afford, or to put together even if funds are unlimited.

But what will be possible, and in many ways a great deal more fun for collectors, is to narrow in on one precise area of fascination, or on one school of photography. Collectors in other fields have done this. There are those who go after American primitives, French Louis XIV furniture, English Georgian silver. Photography collectors of today will find it a great deal more challenging and mentally quickening to do the same—to become specialists.

And to come to grips with the constantly nagging question of the negative, as well.

4 | How to Be Positive About a Negative

THE FACTS ABOUT INVESTING IN A SEEMINGLY INFINITE ITEM

"What should matter is not how many copies of a photograph were printed, but whether the image was worth printing at all."

—ALAN FERN, Library of Congress

OF ALL THE MYRIAD QUESTIONS CONFRONTING THE POTENTIAL NEW photography collector, none is more perplexing than the issue of the negative, the individual recording of a photographer's composition on a roll of film. Technically, it is possible that an unlimited number of prints of the picture can be made from it, provided, of course, that it isn't lost or damaged.

And this is what bothers so many people. Dealers freely admit that it is inevitably the first question they must answer satisfactorily when working with new clients. The plain truth is, the majority of people cannot resist thinking, even subconsciously, that art is an investment. And because we are all taught the law of supply and demand—rare items become more valuable while mass-produced goods do not—the supposedly unlimited supply of prints from a negative bothers most novice collectors.

"Where does that put photographs as an investment?" they ask. "What happens to the value of my print of *Eggplant #19* when the photographer decides to print a hundred more copies of it?" a collector rightly wants to know.

It puts the mystery of the negative into the same historic perspective as the flight of the bumblebee. Scientifically, this two-winged insect should not be able to get off the ground—or at least that was what the world thought for a long time. "But we have recently revised the law of aerodynamics," says Alice Gray of the American Museum of Natural History, "and the result is, the bumblebee can now fly. We can prove it mathematically! It was a case of a fact *forcing* the correction of an obvious error."

Setting the Record Straight about the Negative

The same is true with photographic negatives. Yes, a quantum number of prints "can" be printed from a negative. But it is a mistake to believe they are. Ansel Adams estimates that he's printed 350 copies of *Moonrise, Hernandez.* He's probably set a record! Most photography curators estimate that five to ten prints made by a photographer from one negative is normal, perhaps even too high a guesstimate. Often it's only one.

Why? Because personalized printing (as opposed to commercial laboratory printing, which most collectors scorn) is hard work, taking a good deal of time and therefore preventing the photographer from going out to make new pictures. "I want to go on record that photographers hate to go back and print old images," says Lee Witkin.* "Far from making dozens, or hundreds, of prints of one image, it's difficult to get them to print at all. I'm sick of the theory that the negative can be printed endlessly. That's theory, not fact."

Peter Bunnell in *The Print Collector's Newsletter* stressed the same thing. "The mistake most commonly made [about photography] is that since there is no limit on the number of prints obtainable from a single negative—vast numbers of prints must exist. Conceptually and in terms of any physical deterioration of the negative, this is true. But in actual practice, this capacity for unlimitedness is not pursued, and a study of the more recent history of photography clearly proves that most photographs would be described as rare. Reasons for this are numerous. The

---

* Faul, Roberta, "For the Collector of Photographs," *Museum News* (Jan./Feb. 1976).

BERENICE ABBOTT (1898–   ). *Canyon, Broadway and Exchange Place,*
N.Y.C., 1936 (Graphics International, Ltd./Lunn Gallery and Marlborough
Gallery).

One of the best known early women photographers, Abbott concentrated on
New York during the 1930s under the auspices of the Federal Art Project.

BRASSAÏ (1899–   ) *La Belle de Nuit,* 1933 (Graphics International, Ltd./ Lunn Gallery).

Henry Miller called Brassaï the "eye of Paris." Indeed, his photographs of the underside of the French capital's nightlife during the 1920s prove that a photographer can be a voyeur.

most important is the photographer's compelling motivation to pursue his creative vision with the camera and not pursue printmaking as an end in itself.

"The majority of photographs derive from this pictorial mode, and when one considers how different this is from the 'inventive' process of the printmaker in other media, the point becomes clear. Frequently a photographer will make only one or two prints from a given negative, and apart from specific requests for an exhibition or purchase, these prints may be the only examples in existence. Such requests are often limited in their number, and from my experience, they are far fewer —even at their most numerous—than the present-day editions being established by other printmakers," Bunnell continues. "The key point is, of course, that there is no declaration of the number of prints produced. Unless the negative is destroyed, the potential to have additional prints will always exist. The death of the photographer establishes one form of guarantee—that no further prints will be made by his hand. Then it is up to scholarship to establish how many prints existed to that point." *

Some Photographers Avoid, Others Enjoy Printing

Printmaking is so time-consuming that some photographers, Cartier-Bresson and Lartigue among them, have *never* printed their own work. Instead, they have carefully supervised assistants who have been sent into the darkroom for this exacting work. Frequently the photographers sign the print afterward, thus giving their approval of their assistants' workmanship. But other photographers, like Ansel Adams, delight in the printing process and will sometimes take a day, perhaps more, to work on one print. "I would go crazy if each print was to be identical to all the others," the master photographer said. "Fortunately, with each print, variations can be made, improvements rendered. Because of this fact, I survive."

* Bunnell, Peter, "Observations on Collecting Photographs," *The Print Collector's Newsletter,* vol. II, no. 2 (May/June 1971).

Teacher and photographer Ray Metzker explains his own enthusiasm for printmaking. "To make a print is to work out a game plan," he says. "I decide what the critical areas are and then, through exposure, I test each one of these areas. It is like the conductor going through a piece with the orchestra and saying to the cello section, 'Look, you are not doing this properly—let us go through it again.' Then they go on to another section. Then they finally take it through in its entirety and that is what printing is all about. The final print has unity and it has tension. It is the tension between the parts that gives it excitement, and it is that overall unity that says it is complete."

Certainly one of the reasons that many photographers didn't print up large numbers of individual prints during their lifetimes was that the public (until now, anyway) didn't buy that many photographs in the first place. As recently as 1973, for instance, Aaron Siskind was quoted as saying, "In all of my years, I don't think I've sold, of the most popular of my prints, ten copies . . . and that's a lot." *

Siskind could take solace in the fact that Edward Weston's best-selling print during his lifetime was *Pepper #30.* He sold twelve of them.

Collectors Prefer Prints Made by Photographer

Now that has changed, of course. And photographers are beginning to complain that they are asked to spend too much time in the darkroom. That is because knowledgeable collectors insist on prints by the photographers themselves. Why? For the same reason you wouldn't tear out an illustration from a book, hang it on your wall, and say it was a collectable photograph. A print made by its creator shortly after it was taken and signed by him or her is the most desirable photograph, the majority of connoisseurs agree. Since printmaking is an integral part of the photographic process, with constant variations of light and dark or color intensity possible, collectors generally favor images in which they believe

---

* "Photographs & Professionals: A Discussion," *The Print Collector's Newsletter,* vol. 4, no. 3 (July/August, 1973), p. 56.

GEORGE HOYNINGEN-HUENE (1900–1968). *Toumanova,* ca. 1940 (Sotheby Parke Bernet, Inc.).

Photographs by commercial artists such as Hoyningen-Huene are becoming increasingly more collectable as statements of the era in which they were done. Hoyningen-Huene was one of Condé Nast's stars on *Vogue,* joining its staff in Paris in 1925. He later joined the staff of *Harper's Bazaar* in New York City in 1935.

they have the greatest input of the artist shortly after conceiving the idea. Because the photograph was presumably taken with the techniques of the craft as well as the materials required to print it in mind, prints made years later, while often very desirable, still cannot be thought of in the same light as the "vintage" one.

To understand why, "to understand how these processes relate to the photographer's pictorial vision, and subsequently to the reputation of a collection's quality and selectivity, demands considerable knowledge and expertise," says Princeton's Peter Bunnell. "For example, a modern silver print made from a negative taken in 1923, but originally conceived to be printed on platinum paper, bears only a partial relationship to the original or first print. Platinum paper is no longer commercially available and thus circumstance, quite outside of the photographer's control, establishes a singular rarity for the first print. Conscious collectors should first seek out the 1923 print. Each print must be considered on its own terms, and the uniqueness of printing or the additional variants of cropping and presentation can only be detected by careful scholarship." *

A good eye can often tell if a print was *even* made by the photographer. Edward Weston, for instance—like some other photographers—had key idiosyncrasies in printing that a scholar can detect after years of examining his original prints. It should be noted, however, that many of Edward Weston's negatives are printed today by his son, Cole, and are identified as such. So are Berenice Abbott's prints of Atget's negatives, and Lee Friedlander's prints of E. J. Bellocq's work. Buying a group of about eighty old glass negatives of New Orleans prostitutes taken about 1912, Friedlander, a noted photographer in his own right, has given collectors a continuing chance to include an image from this "Toulouse-Lautrec of photography."

But not everyone wishes to buy one. "If I want the work of a particular photographer, I want the print to be by him, too," says a demanding collector. "The taking of an image and the printing of an image are too

---

* Bunnell, Peter, "Observations on Collecting Photographs," *The Print Collector's Newsletter,* vol. II, no. 2 (May/June, 1971).

ARTHUR H. FELLIG ("Weegee") (1899–1969). *Marilyn Monroe,* ca. 1953 (Graphics International, Ltd./Lunn Gallery).

A news photographer, Weegee worked at night to cover fires, murders, and other early-hour mishaps. When not rushing to the scene of a crime, he did assignments for *Vogue, Life,* and *Look.* A self-promoter, he stamped his prints "Weegee the Famous."

---

closely interwoven to be separated and still come out with a worthwhile work of art. I think that a photograph taken by X and printed by Y is not the same thing as one taken by and printed by X. Anyone who thinks differently is kidding himself. No two people print alike. Face it! The very fact that there's a price difference between an image taken and printed by X and one taken by X and printed by Y proves my point. Thank God there are enough people who see the difference that the market reflects the truth."

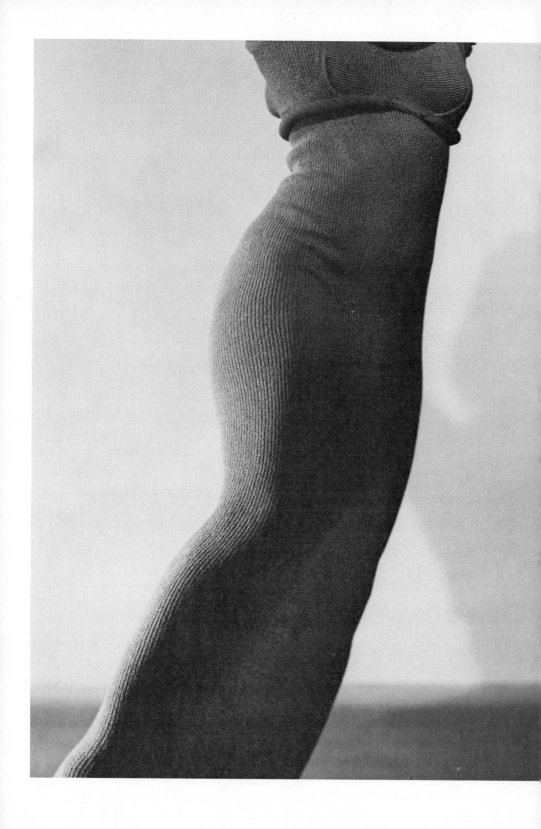

Forgeries and Fakes

Forgeries are something else, however. While not an issue of major importance at this time, it is an area that Peter Bunnell, director of the Princeton University Art Museum, feels should be watched carefully by dealers and collectors. "About forgeries and fakes, I've seen some mis-attributed photographs, but that's not the same thing," he says. "And I've seen some forged signatures. This is more serious. I saw a photograph supposedly signed by the artist, for instance, the other day. It wasn't. I've seen too many of the photographer's genuine signatures not to be able to tell the difference. Someone figured he'd add value to the print by faking a signature.

"Forgery isn't a real problem, yet, though," he continues. "There is still enough material available and the prices are generally low enough still that there isn't an incentive yet to resort to forgery. But as some photographers' pictures run out, we may be in for trouble. I'd like to say, however, that the first step toward forgery is beginning with the sale of unsigned prints that vaguely look like the work of famous photographers. At a recent auction, for instance, there was a photograph 'attributed' to Steichen. It looked like his. But who knows for sure if it *really* is his?"

Limited-Edition Portfolios Grow in Number

One aspect of the photography market that has accelerated but that has gone on for years is the production of limited-edition portfolios. It is a selection of the artist's images that he and/or his dealer feel best repre-

---

BARBARA MORGAN (1900–   ). *Martha Graham, "Ekstasis,"* 1935 (Collection of the artist).

Conscious that the world is in perpetual motion, Morgan is fascinated with modern dance. For five years, she focused on Martha Graham. The results enthrall collectors who delight in the photographer's ability "to fuse dance action, light and space simultaneously. . . ."

sent either his current and/or his retrospective eye. Normally each print is signed and numbered to indicate its authenticity and its position within a printing. For instance, "3/100" would mean the purchaser was getting the third print in an edition of 100. It is the same technique used in limited editions of other graphics.

The greatest number of any photograph ever printed would rarely come close to the least amount of the most insignificant graphic, which makes photographs all the more intriguing.

Today, photographers such as Ansel Adams, Eva Rubinstein, Paul Caponigro, George Tice, Arthur Tress, Leslie Krims, Lilo Raymond, Brett Weston, Roman Vishniac, Geoff Winningham, and Elliott Erwitt are among those who practice the portfolio marketing technique. With each photographer, the size of the edition will vary, of course. But in very few cases is there a contractual agreement with the portfolio's publisher (galleries for the most part) that no future prints in the portfolio will ever again be made. Few photographers wish to limit their earning power from a particularly successful photograph in such a way, by taking an arbitrary number out of the air and saying it is to be the extent of the image's production.

What in fact is normally stated, as a recent advertisement of George Tice's *Portfolio V* in the September, 1976, issue of *Artforum* demonstrates, is that the photographs "will not be printed in the same manner again." The opportunity, therefore, for the photographer to print the images on different paper, in a different style, with different dimensions: all these options remain open.

ANSEL ADAMS (1902–   ). *White Stump,* Sierra Nevada, c. 1936, from Portfolio V published by Parasol Press, N.Y.C., 1971 (Graphics International, Ltd./ Lunn Gallery).

Technical perfection and grandeur typify Adams' photographs. Prices for his images rose dramatically in 1976 when the 75-year-old master ceased taking new print orders to complete his long-standing back orders.

Collector Questions So-called
Limited-Edition Portfolio

It is this aspect of the portfolio that bothers collector Frank K. "I don't really like the so-called limited-edition portfolio," he says. " 'This is one of a hundred.' And then the photographer can subsequently print 5,000 of the individual images in the portfolio a quarter of an inch larger and be okay. So don't call it a 'limited edition.' To me a limited edition implies that every single image in that portfolio is limited to the number of the portfolio. Say to me, instead, 'Look, we've put together a group of photographs by a particular artist and we've made a portfolio.' That's all."

Time-Life has now gotten into the act, too. Only they have returned to the past. At a cost of $150 apiece, the company is selling 2,500 editions of a "Mathew Brady's Great Americans" series, which includes Lincoln, Kit Carson, Longfellow, and P. T. Barnum. About these sets of prints made from Brady's glass negatives in the Meserve Collection, the publishers say that no other editions will ever be made from these negatives again. Each photograph has been archivally processed, a technique demanded by knowledgeable collectors in order to remove as much acid as possible from the paper and thus extend its longevity.

One of the reasons that portfolios are popular with photographers today is that they make money—often big money. At $1,600 apiece, 75 sets of George Tice's *Portfolio II* sold within eight weeks, thus grossing $120,000! At the same time, portfolios make decision-making easy for collectors. Their minds are made up for them about which images by a photographer to buy, including those contained in a portfolio issued in 1976, advertised in *The New York Times* and pure Americana in scope.

Entitled "Down Home—Plains, Georgia," the body of work presented mail-order purchasers with a look at President Jimmy Carter's hometown, including views of the Skylight Night Club, Neil's Sandwich Shop, the Carter Worm Farm, the Plains Post Office, and Cousin Hugh Carter's Antique Shop.

Whether it, too, will become a collector's item is anyone's guess, but chances are that it will. In photography collecting, like in politics, new directions are being traveled every day.

5 | The Care and Feeding of Black and White Photographs

CONSERVATION AND RESTORATION

"I am now with Light Gallery. I am an adjunct teacher at the
Rhode Island School of Design. The Center for Creative Photography
at the University of Arizona has purchased my archives.
Anybody want my bones?"

—AARON SISKIND

MUSEUM CURATORS OF PHOTOGRAPHY WOULD BE HORRIFIED TO SEE how and where a well-known collector stores his prints of great historical interest. They are under his bed, stacked one upon the other and in no container whatsoever. This individual may feel that what to some would be considered irreverent handling of the photographs allows for the spirit of spontaneity of a collector with a cache, like the little old lady with a million dollars stuffed in her mattress. In this spirit the gentleman drags out a few prints each morning, props them up on the back of a sofa, and revels in his images over coffee before going to work.

This collector blithely ignores standard rules of conservation, meaning the proper storage and handling of photographs to ensure that they remain in their current condition.

Eugene Ostroff, curator of photography at the Smithsonian Institution and an authority on the conservation and restoration of photographic materials, writes: "Ideally, thorough conservation of photographs requires complete removal of all residual chemicals and gold toning, and storage in an inert atmosphere maintained at 50% relative humidity, 50° F, within a sterilized, stainless steel container that is sealed by weld-

ing. Obviously, this is an impractical approach, one that requires some compromises. . . ." *

Indeed, nobody with a normal approach to collecting would allow photographs to be welded out of sight in a stainless-steel box. The question therefore becomes: What are the optimum conditions the average collector should provide for his or her photographs?

Conservatorial Procedures

First of all, to be on the safe side, anyone collecting vintage material, or the photographs of someone who might have been unaware of the potential collectability of the work, should have prints checked by a qualified restorer for residual chemicals left on them as the result of inadequate darkroom procedures. A respected restorer, José Oracca, says, "It's important to consider the craftsmanship of the individual photographer. For example, if you want to buy a Lewis Hine photograph, or even a Walker Evans, you know that these prints will have to be rewashed. These men's washing procedures were really not the best. You have to know about a photographer, but it would be very difficult for the average collector to tell."

Hine, Evans, and others did not willfully neglect darkroom standards that ensure a print life for hundreds of years. They probably had no idea that such standards would become vital in the future. However, most contemporary photographers involved in the art photography marketplace are fastidious about their darkroom work.

* Ostroff, Eugene, "Conserving and Restoring Photographic Collections," *Museum News* (May, 1974), p. 42.

WALKER EVANS (1903–1976). *Wellfleet, Mass.,* 1931 (Sotheby Parke Bernet, Inc.).

The signature of an artist can increase prices for his work, including photographs. The five seconds it took Evans to sign this print on the lower right adds several hundreds of dollars to its value. It is from a limited edition of 100 prints.

Ostroff confirms the need to be so. "Photographic collections are extremely vulnerable to the effects of residual chemicals. If the chemicals used in processing are not completely removed from the photograph, the image gradually will deteriorate and eventually will be destroyed. . . . Prints appearing to be in good condition may, years later, begin to stain and fade." *

Beyond having questionable prints rewashed, a collector can further insure photographs from fading by having them "toned," a process that all responsible contemporary photographers include in their darkroom procedures. The process involves coating the metallic silver emulsion of the print with gold, selenium, or sepia toner. There is a question, however, as to the propriety of toning prints of deceased photographers. The process creates a caste or hue, which might not be consonant with a photographer's intentions or aesthetic sense.

Mounting and Matting

Nonetheless, having stopped all chemical activity, or confident that there is none, the collector will want to mount, mat, possibly frame, and properly store the photographs. Presentation of photographs has been fairly standardized. The main reason for a lack of latitude is that there are few materials—papers, boards, frames, adhesives, tapes, and so on—that are proven to be chemically inert, and therefore safe to be in contact with photographs. That is why one sees most photographs in galleries and museums presented simply, in white mats and metal frames.

Collectors should mount and mat their photographs to avoid having to handle the image itself. Touching the image surface is absolutely taboo, as fingerprints leave salt that eventually bleaches the photograph.

Only 100 percent cotton-rag "museum board" should be used for mounting and matting. Inferior-quality wood-pulp boards, made from compressed layers with adhesives between them, are not acid-free. If the photograph is to be preserved, these boards should not be used.

* Ibid., p. 40.

AARON SISKIND (1903–   ). *Kentucky,* 1951 (Collection of the Museum of Modern Art).

What is so special about taking photographs of graffiti, torn posters, and chipping plaster? For Siskind ". . . subject-matter, as such, ceased to be of primary importance." When one sees his images one realizes that it is not what is photographed, but how it is photographed that puts Siskind in the same league with many contemporary painters.

The print is sandwiched between the mount board, or backboard, which supports the photograph, and a top board, or mat, in which a window is cut to frame the image.

There is some disagreement as to the best method of affixing the print to the backboard. Ansel Adams and others use dry-mount tissue, which holds the print flat and is sealed by heat. Some conservators question whether dry-mount tissue is chemically inert over long periods of time, but it definitely provides the neatest presentation.

However, if a collector buys a print of a contemporary photographer that is dry-mounted, he or she should make sure that the print is toned and is on 100 percent rag board. This will avoid problems in the future of having to separate the print from the backboard for conservatorial treatment.

Some conservators feel that it is best to hinge the print to the backboard, preferably with Japanese mulberry paper or gummed linen tape. Scotch, masking, or other pressure-adhesive tapes should be avoided. So should rubber cement and spray adhesives, which often contain sulfur, iron, copper, or other ingredients that may attack image emulsion, gelatin, or the paper support of prints.

According to Ostroff, "Very few commercial products are tailored to meet the needs of photographic collectors. The requirements for all these materials are numerous and very specific. Perhaps, consumers have not made their needs fully known to the manufacturers, who might still feel that the market potential, as yet, is too weak to justify producing such highly specialized products." *

Nonetheless, once prints are properly mounted and matted, they should never be stacked one upon the other without the protection of an acid-free "cover sheet" over the image and beneath the mat. Among the materials recommended for cover sheets are delicate sheets of Japanese tissue, cellulose triacetates, and uncoated polyesters such as Mylar-D. They are transparent, and collectors can order them in sheets of varying sizes and thicknesses. These sheets minimize the possibility of abrasion from dirt particles.

* Ibid., p. 36.

If for some reason mounting and matting prints is undesirable, the photographs should at least be kept with cover sheets between them. Glassine and other paper envelopes for unmounted prints are considered a liability, especially because of the gummed seams, which are not acid-free. And brown kraft or manila envelopes contain image-damaging ingredients as well. Over long periods of time, these materials become brittle and disintegrate. It is advisable not to get into the habit of using them, even "temporarily." Transparent plastic print envelopes are widely used, but these should be kept in a low-humidity environment, as they can become moisture traps. At any rate, do not affix annotated self-adhesive labels to the back of the prints. The collective weight of the stacked prints with raised labels may cause indentations on the images. And wet labels pucker eventually.

As for framing, molded or sectional metal frames are the preferred type because they are aesthetically neat and durable and the material is inert. Bleached, fresh, or varnished wood frames should not be used. Woods embody destructive peroxide called "lignin." They can be finished with a permanent wood sealer, but there may be danger even then.

Glass has fallen out of favor, too, because of its weight and breakage factors. Splintered glass could severely damage emulsions. And nonreflecting glass flattens the tonality of the image. Therefore, although it is softer and susceptible to scratching, unbreakable, lightweight Plexiglas is often used. It can be ordered with a built-in shield against ultraviolet light. However, the glass or Plexiglas should not be in direct contact with the print surface. There should be a mat separating the two so that the print can breathe. A narrow rag board strip fitted under the rabbet (front edge) of the frame can also form an adequate separator.

There are purists, however, who feel that a photograph should not be covered by a shiny glass or Plexiglas surface at all. Not only is there a reflection problem, but these people feel that the glass is an unwanted artificial element between the viewer and the "reality" of the image. Such people may be tempted to spray the surface of prints to protect them against fingerprinting. Ansel Adams recommends the use of clear plastic Krylon spray.

But Ostroff warns, "Don't use plastic sprays on your photographs. These

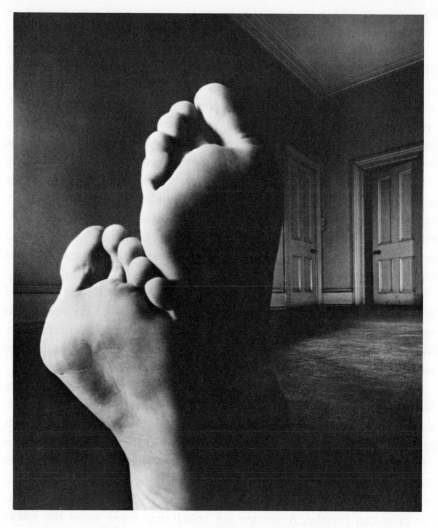

BILL BRANDT (1904–   ). *Feet,* 1952 and 1956 (Marlborough Gallery).

Perhaps the most respected photographer in England today, Bill Brandt, like many of the world's best-known photographers, often is capable of working in many different styles. A documentary and portrait photographer, as well as a Surrealist, he often superimposes portions of nude bodies floating in empty rooms or against landscapes.

acrylic resins, varnishes and lacquers might contain solvents, catalysts, or impurities that attack the image during long-term storage. With age, they might discolor, become tacky and ooze, or be affected by gaseous contaminants or unfavorable variations of temperature and humidity." *

There is also a debate as to whether framed photographs should be sealed with paper from the back to keep out contaminants. Doing so prohibits the prints from breathing, some authorities believe.

Storage

Storage of unframed but mounted and matted prints is the next step that collectors should consider. Most photographs not actually on display in frames, either in private homes or museums, should be responsibly contained. Naturally the average collector will not have special storage rooms, as do many museums, with "anodized aluminum, steel with baked-on nonplasticized synthetic resin lacquer, or stainless-steel cabinets," as one curator recommends. Therefore, under the bed may be about the best the average photography collector may be able to do.

But mounted, matted prints should at least be kept in solander boxes. These are made of light, well-seasoned wood, covered with fabric and lined with acid-free paper. The lid closes over a dust flange, and the box is usually fastened by clasps. When open, the lid falls flat on the table, forming a tray. Prints can be easily transferred from box to lid and back again with a minimum of movement.

There are some strict conservators who would even doubt the safety of the solander box, because it is made of wood that is known to exude acid. But these boxes are widely used on all levels of photographic and print collecting.

To find out where to buy solander boxes and other materials for mounting, matting, and framing photographs, ask local galleries or the photographic departments of the nearest museum. There is also a list of suppliers that manufacture materials to conservatorial specifications in Appendix 3 of this book.

* Ibid., p. 45.

Optimum Environment for Storage

Having taken all these recommendations into consideration, collectors then need to provide as cool and dry an environment for their photographs as they can. This may necessitate a dehumidifier in southern climates, where humidity causes fungus growths. The hazards of sea air can also be lessened by dehumidification.

High air-pollution levels are a danger to photographic prints, too, but these are generally out of a collector's control. There is one time when they are not, though; this is when the apartment or house is being painted.

Avoid storing prints, especially newly processed ones less than six months old, in freshly painted rooms. Wait three to four weeks for fumes to dissolve. Paint fumes and fresh chemistry on photographic prints react badly to each other.

Collectors should be on the alert for vermin, too. Cockroaches, termites, silverfish and woodworms love to eat paper.

For people toying with the idea of starting a photographic collection, the thought of having to protect their prints against bugs as well as maintain the standard conservatorial procedures may make the collecting activity seem more a nuisance than a joy. But, as Doris Bry, manager of the Stieglitz estate, affirms, "The enumeration of so many hazards to photographs should not discourage the enthusiastic collector, but rather, should stimulate him to take the best possible care of his acquisitions." *

Shortage of Trustworthy Restorers

The foregoing conservatorial precautions are to protect photographs from deterioration. They "permanentize" the image, a term common in the 1800s. However, if a collector has a photograph, tintype, daguerreotype, or ambrotype that is in need of restoration, of having its condition improved, he or she is up against the same challenge that top dealers have been contending with for years. "The fact is," says restorer-consultant

---

* Bry, Doris, *An Approach to the Care of Photographs* (New York: Sotheby Parke Bernet, 1976).

MARGARET BOURKE-WHITE (1904–1971). *Louisville Flood Victims,* 1937 (Time-Life Picture Agency).

One of the first female photographers to establish a "name" for herself, Bourke-White worked for *Fortune* magazine and later for *Life.* She was a prime contributor to early photojournalism, an area of growing interest to collectors.

———————————

Murray Duitz, "The dealers are at just as much of a loss for qualified, skilled restorers of photographic materials as are the private collectors."

The prime reason for the dearth of restorers is that there has been, until recently, little demand for the work. Only in the last five years have photographs been considered a collectable art form and therefore worth restoring.

There is also growing interest in the medium by academics. As Os-

troff says, "Photographs are a disappearing legacy unless they have proper care. . . . Scholars have shown a growing interest in using early photographs as a primary source of reference. . . . Photographs which enable readers to personally witness the past are now, more than ever, generously used by authors and publishers to lend validity to themes, spur reader imagination and brighten otherwise dreary presentations." *

Inadequate Scientific Data

Ostroff then goes on to explain added complications, which only time will resolve, in the science of photographic preservation. "Man-made papers have existed since about the second century, A.D. By analyzing the state of preservation of these papers and their construction, we may obtain a great deal of useful information. The short history of photography, however, fails to allow parallel studies of 'natural' long-term aging.

"The problems and possible answers involving preservation of photographs are vastly more complicated than those concerning plain papers. Photographs are multilayer constructions of different materials—organic and inorganic—and the interaction of these products under a wide variety of storage and handling conditions greatly complicates analytical procedures. Most of this information must be extracted from artificially aged material, manufactured by accelerated 'aging' methods in the laboratory. Information derived from these tests is not always reliable." †

* Ostroff, op. cit., p. 34.

† Ostroff, op. cit. p. 42.

CLARENCE JOHN LAUGHLIN (1905–   ). *The Haunting Gaze,* 1941 (Graphics International, Ltd./Lunn Gallery).

While psychological and introspective photography became popular in the 1970s among young photographers, Laughlin has been exploring the mental realm since he took up photography in 1935.

First Formal Conservatorial Program

Despite the lack of concrete scientific data on conservation and the shortage of skilled restorers, there is a well-known restorer, José Oracca, who is doing all he can to meet the need of preserving our photographic legacy.

Oracca began in the fall of 1976 a three-year program on the conservation of photographs at the University of Delaware. The scientific aspects of the course are taught at the university and the practical applications are taught at the facilities of the renowned Winterthur Program for the Conservation of Artistic and Historic Works.

"It is the only formal program in the country," Oracca says. "We have received a tremendous amount of inquiries and applications for the course. But our requirements are very stringent. For example, we require extensive background in both chemistry and art history. Many of the students will have to do remedial work. But there is a tremendous interest in the course, which is very satisfying to me and to the university because we feel rewarded for our commitment."

Unfortunately, Oracca's teaching makes him generally inaccessible to dealers and collectors for restoration work.

"I have many requests to do restoration and a backlog of photographs that need attention. I could easily devote full time to the work. But if I do that, it will still be just me. I really feel that my greatest contribution to the medium is to get the weight off my shoulders by teaching and turning out new conservators. And I must do it quickly, because unqualified people are getting into the business."

Indeed, there are some horror stories of naïve collectors, and even dealers, who have entrusted valuable photographs to unskilled and unknowledgeable restorers. There are several instances when people have taken short courses from museum conservation departments or from restorers. Then, with no practical experience, they will have business cards made and open up shop. Irreparable damage has been done in some cases.

As Oracca says, "The possibility of damage by an untrained restorer is even higher in photography than in painting or any other medium.

If the restorer doesn't know the difference between a gelatin print and a collodion print, he could give it completely wrong treatment. It takes analysis and a real knowledge of the many photographic processes throughout the medium's history to know what you've got in your hands."

Upcoming Guide to Photographers' Practices

Another contribution Oracca plans to make is a guide to the photographic processing practices of well-known photographers. This information will be based on his familiarity with their work. He intends to explain how these people mounted, washed, and otherwise treated their prints. This will be of invaluable help to dealers, collectors, and other restorers in knowing what kind of conservatorial treatment a photograph may need.

"For example," Oracca points out, "if you buy an Alvarez Bravo photograph, you should know that he mounted his prints, for the most part, with rubber cement which is going to bleach the image. Some of them are already bleaching. Or if you get a Talbot calotype, you will know that it may be fading because it was mounted with animal adhesive. I want to compile as much of this kind of information into a source guide as I can."

Apart from learning what to be on the alert for with a given photographer's prints, Oracca has also become aware of some little-known shenanigans in the art photography world.

"Stieglitz and Strand used photographs that were not good prints, throwaway prints, maybe one or two, as backings for their original photographs. They did this to raise them from the mounts. They liked the way this looked. Now, many times a collector or dealer will take them apart, use a solvent to dissolve the adhesive, and sell the prints separately, all as top-quality, photographer-approved originals. Of course, the photographers never intended for these to be sold. They probably didn't even know that people would be 'profiting' from their work. If they did, they surely would have thrown these seconds away."

This is the type of information Oracca hopes to impart to as many students as possible, as well as training them in the practical applications of restoration. Unfortunately, it will be three years until the first gradua-

HORST P. HORST (1906–   ). *Coco Chanel,* 1936 (Sonnabend Gallery).
A member of Gertrude Stein's circle of friends in Paris, Horst was originally
a fashion photographer. He is better known today as a creative recorder of the
well-to-do. This portrait of Coco Chanel is Horst's own favorite among his
many portraits.

tion day from his course, and probably a couple more in apprenticeships before his fledglings are ready to fly professionally. Until then, and until restorers emerge from elsewhere, there will be a shortage of fully experienced, qualified people in the field.

Where Do Collectors Turn?

According to Walter Clark, consultant to the new Conservation Center at the International Museum of Photography at George Eastman House, "Even the conservation laboratories of the great museums and galleries have very little experience in this field." * The Conservation Center is primarily devoted to the preservation of its own collection, but Alice Swann, the conservator, is willing to field questions from individual collectors on the care, storage, and restoration of photographs.

Collectors can also query galleries, museums with photography collections, and the American National Standards Institute in New York City. This organization has on file the consensus of standards for photographic processes and materials.

Also willing to receive questions on restoration are José Oracca, at the University of Delaware, Newark, Delaware, and Murray Duitz, a restorer-consultant, in Baldwin, New York, who, owing to the demand from galleries, has recently begun doing full-time restoration work.

But, because the field of restoration and conservation is so new, it is wise to weigh people's recommendations against others before taking action.

It would also be helpful to do some further reading on the preservation of photographic materials. For a list of useful reference sources, see Appendix 2 in this book.

But unfortunately there is very little practical advice to give collectors about restoration. If you have photographs in need of treatment, and you find a restorer willing to take on the job, be 100 percent sure he has had

---

* Clark, Walter, "Techniques for Conserving Those Old Photographs," *The New York Times* (June 3, 1976), p. 37.

GEORGE PLATT LYNES (1907–1955). *Diogenes & Alexander,* ca. 1945 (Sonnabend Gallery).

Lynes photographed nudes, fashion, and made portraits of writers and artists. He enjoyed, as well, photographing ballet dancers and illustrating mythological tales.

---

prior experience and knows what he is doing. You may wish to ask for some references.

Also, be sure to ask the dealer from whom you are buying the photograph if it has had any conservatorial attention. You cannot assume that it has. If, however, the print needs treatment, or at least rewashing, you may want to weigh conservation costs against the print price. According to Murray Duitz, $25 an hour is about standard for restorers. Actually, there are some collectors who have learned to do their own rewashing.

However, as a preliminary precaution, it's always good to know something about the provenance of a photograph you may buy. Most damage to prints is the result of haphazard handling by previous owners rather than inadequate processing by the photographer.

The Value of Restoration

To leave the subject of restoration and conservation on a promising note for dealers and collectors alike, consider two cheery tales involving people who managed to find restorers for a print and a daguerreotype bought in bad condition.

A sharp dealer spotted a badly stained Stieglitz print at an auction. It was merely in need of a good washing to remove residual chemistry. He got the print for a low price, other bidders being leery of its condition. He then had it washed, a simple, inexpensive operation, and resold the print at a handsome profit.

But most dealers will avoid buying prints in serious need of retouching and restoration. Generally, by the time the work is done and paid for, the profit margin is low.

A private collector can do well, too. A man bought a daguerreotype at a flea market for $2.00. The glass in the case, which served to protect the image from the air, had been lost. Consequently the image had oxidized and was barely visible. Restoration revealed the portrait of President Franklin Pierce. The daguerreotype commanded over $1,000 upon resale.

Stories such as these show the advantages of and need for restoration and conclusive conservatorial guidelines. There will be no shortage of photographs to be preserved in the future. People are no longer throwing them away, oblivious to their potential value.

"I've tossed out endless daguerreotypes, tintypes, and cartes-de-visite over the years," exclaimed an antique dealer in Savannah. "I found them in drawers of almost every piece of furniture I bought. But I've had ten people in here after photographs in the last couple of months. I won't be throwing them away anymore!"

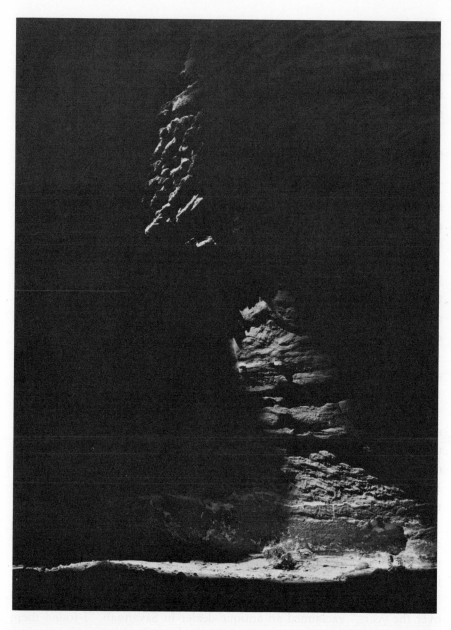

MINOR WHITE (1908–1976). *Light on a Canyon Wall,* Capitol Reef, 1962
(The Photographic Gallery, Columbia College, Chicago, Ill.).

Considered one of America's most intellectual photographers, White was
deeply interested in religion and philosophy. A professor of creative photography
at M.I.T., White's own work presents a mystical dimensionality.

Indeed, people from Savannah to San Francisco are realizing that photography is no longer the stepchild of the arts. Today it is a full-blooded sibling. Because of this, there will no doubt be increased attention paid to the field of restoration and conservation of photographic art work in the immediate years to come.

6 | The Compromise of Color

NEW PROCESSES AND WHETHER TO INVEST

"How long will a color print last? Longer than most marriages."
—VICTOR SCHRAGER, Light Gallery

THROUGHOUT THE HISTORY OF CIVILIZATION, PEOPLE HAVE RECORDED in color their sense of reality. Stone Age man left clues to his life-style on cave walls, the Etruscans decorated tombs with natural dyes, and Quattrocento Italian painters left frescoes of great beauty on church walls and ceilings. The French Impressionists upset the traditional, subdued color standards of nineteenth-century academic art with their soft pastels and giddy color combinations. Modern artists of today introduce an even broader scale of acceptable color to the increasingly tolerant eyes of art appreciators. It seems as if color photography, too, is on the threshold of acceptability, with growing numbers of collectors, both private and institutional. Color photographer Stephen Shore said, "I'm fascinated by the world I see, and it happens to be in color. Color is not irrelevant to this world. It is as resonant as any other factor."

Color: What Is It?

Not only did Sir Isaac Newton discover calculus and the law of gravity, but he also demonstrated that light was the source of color. This discovery in 1666, that light is composed of all the colors in the spectrum, was the kick-off to establishing fundamentals of color and how it is reproduced photographically.

By dictionary definition, color is "that quality of an object by which it emits, reflects or transmits certain rays of light and absorbs others, thus producing a specific effect on the eye, depending on the nature of the rays reaching the nervous elements of the retina, the immediate stimulus of which is photochemical."

The question of color photography's collectability excited the nervous system of the photography world in 1976 with the color show of William Eggleston's work at the Museum of Modern Art in New York. The show revived a two-pronged question, the first being technical, the second aesthetic. Collectors considering color photographs should be familiar with both issues.

Fugitive Color

First, the fugitive nature of color prints has haunted the medium since its inception. That spectrum colors could be impressed on paper and impregnated with silver chloride was the discovery of a German physicist, Johann Seebeck, in 1810. But experimenters such as Edmond Becquerel, Sir John Herschel, the French lithographer Joseph-Nicéphore Niépce, and an American Baptist minister, Levi L. Hill, also contributed with varying success to the quest for a colorfast image.

Niépce shared his research with his brother, exclaiming, "But I must succeed in *fixing* the colors." In 1827 Niépce joined forces with Louis Daguerre, soon to be the inventor of the daguerreotype, and wrote to his son: "Monsieur Daguerre has arrived at the point of registering on his chemical substance some of the colored rays of the prism; he has already reunited four and he is working on combining the other three in order to have the seven primary colors. But the difficulties which he encounters grow in proportion to the modification which this same substance must undergo in order to retain several colors at the same time. . . . After what he told me, he has little hope of succeeding." *

---

* Newhall, Beaumont, *The History of Photography* (New York: The Museum of Modern Art, 1964), p. 191.

HARRY CALLAHAN (1912–   ). Untitled, 1957 (Light Gallery).
Callahan is noted for the simplicity of line common to most of his work. He is best known for his elegant studies of nature.

Later, in the 1850s, the Baptist minister Levi L. Hill of Westkill, New York, was making color daguerreotypes, which he called "hillotypes." He seemed to have arrived at an indelible color image but couldn't be persuaded, not even by money, to share his findings with the photographic community, stating that he would disclose his formulas, "when I think it proper." The proper time never came and the minister died in 1865, leaving much speculation as to the validity of his claims.

But the public was obviously longing for natural color portraiture. With the publicity of Hill's alleged discovery, the businesses of professional daguerreotypists fell off considerably. Clients postponed black and

WILLIAM GARNETT (1916–   ). *Sand Dune,* Death Valley, ca. 1954 (Marlborough Gallery).

Many photographers develop a point of view. Garnett's focus originates from the sky. His ærial photographs of the American West are mysterious abstracts of the earth below.

LILO RAYMOND (1922–   ). *Trout,* 1976 (Marcuse Pfeiffer Gallery).
   Classical yet earthy and contemporary are the qualities that describe Raymond's still lifes. She is bravely alone in her love for the still life as subject matter, in a photography world drifting away from classicism.

---

white sittings, awaiting the introduction of color to the portrait studios. Black and white portraits had been hand-tinted to meet the demands for color, but this was, of course, more expensive.

   Abel Niépce de Saint-Victor, Joseph-Nicéphore Niépce's nephew, working at the same time as the Reverend Hill, also succeeded in making color daguerreotypes. But unfortunately he couldn't guarantee their longevity. Only a few examples of his work, preserved in darkness, remain to be seen today.

   In 1861 the English physicist James Clerk Maxwell introduced the additive method of color photography in which a black and white print was the basis. The shades of gray were utilized to control the value of dyes of the primary colors, which were applied to the monochromatic print. The first practical color prints were made by variations of Maxwell's process.

In 1869, two Frenchmen, Louis du Hauron and Charles Cros, each spurred by knowledge of the other's research, announced independently but simultaneously the discovery of the subtractive method, which eventually became the basis for all color photographic processes in the future. In this method, colors were created by combining dyed images, rather than mixing colored lights as was done in Maxwell's additive method. Both processes, however, attempted to reproduce all visible colors by mixing proportions of a few primary colors, not necessarily just three.

In the 1890s, Alphonse Poitevin, Gabriel Lipman, and Professor R. Wood contributed theoretically, but impractically, to natural color photographic processes. But by the first quarter of the twentieth century, photographers including Edward Steichen, Alfred Stieglitz, and Louis Lumière, coinventor with his brother, Auguste, of the Autochrome process, were making hundreds of color pictures, some of which are still visible today. The Autochrome, a derivative of Maxwell's process, utilized colored dots to achieve quite acceptable renditions of reality. It was the most satisfactory process until the introduction of Kodachrome onto the commercial market by the Eastman Kodak Company in 1935.

Musicians Invent Kodachrome

Kodachrome was the first easy-to-use color process for the amateur and professional photographer and is responsible for those cobalt blue skies made ubiquitous by *National Geographic* magazine. Interestingly enough, it was two musicians who provided the world with the film. Leopold

---

ARNOLD NEWMAN (1918–   ). *Jean Dubuffet, 1956* (Light Gallery).
Newman lifts portrait photography out of the recording category and makes it an art form. His thoughtful portraits of famous people frequently suggest their professions.

Mannes and Leopold Godowsky, Jr., were fellow boyhood tinkerers with photography. Mannes was a pianist who later became manager of the famed, family-owned Mannes School of Music in New York City. Godowsky, a violinist, was the son of the internationally known pianist Leopold Godowsky, Sr. Their joint research began in grade school in their families' bathrooms, kitchens, and closets, which proved to be a nuisance for all involved. They were ultimately evicted by their families and had to set up a darkroom in a New York hotel. At one point, they attracted funding to the tune of $20,000 from the Wall Street investment firm of Kuhn, Loeb, and Co.

After many years, their research was drawn to the attention of Dr. C. E. Kenneth Mees, director of research at the Eastman Kodak Company. In 1930 the two men joined the Kodak staff in Rochester, New York, where for the first time they had suitable facilities for experimentation. They pushed on with research by day and entertained friends with their chamber music at night.

On April 15, 1935, Kodak placed Kodachrome on the market. It was the best solution to the century-old search for a practical color process of photography. The positive color transparency was largely the result of Mannes and Godowsky's efforts. Its basis was, however, Hauron's and Cros's subtractive method.

AGFA Secrets Become War Booty

The limelight on Mannes and Godowsky was stolen, however, by AGFA, a German firm, which introduced Afgacolor only a few months after the announcement of Kodachrome. It was a close game of one-upmanship. Agfacolor included color couplers, or formers, in the film emulsion itself, an important development.

But United States soldiers put out the limelight on the AGFA plant toward the end of World War II. "U.S. troops seized the AGFA plant at Wolfen, near Leipzig, Germany, and 'liberated' the closely guarded technical details of the method of making Agfacolor. The patent rights were seized as war indemnity, becoming public property, and the formulas were distributed to film manufacturers around the world. Agfacolor thus became the basis for a variety of color processes, and by the mid 1950s many companies scattered from Italy to Japan were producing high quality, easy-to-use color film for the amateur and professional. . . . By 1964, American amateur photographers were taking more color pictures than black and white." *

Kodak also introduced Ektachrome, which could be processed in amateur darkrooms, providing they were well equipped, and Kodacolor, a negative color film, from which enlargements could be made. Both were once again the result of the research of Mannes and Godowsky, who eventually retired to the music world for good.

In 1962 Edwin H. Land announced Polacolor. The Polaroid Corp. of Cambridge, Massachusetts, now had its color prints in minutes.

This cursory review of more than a century of color photography's history indicates the challenges that the medium has undergone. Unfortunately, the quest for a permanent color print is still under way. Because of the current collectability of photographs, the industry is more concerned than ever with the fugitive nature of color prints. But the problem has been ameliorated increasingly over the decades, to the point where color photography galleries presently entering the marketplace are providing longevity guarantees with color print sales.

Most Indelible Print Type?

At this point in time the question has become: Which is the least fugitive and aesthetically acceptable print type available for collectors of color photographs? Which is least susceptible to fading?

The print process that over the years has been the preferred type by established color photographers is the dye transfer. Robert P. Speck and Louis Condix invented the process, which was put on the commercial market in 1946 through Eastman Kodak. Speck, recently retired from Kodak, now works as a free-lance consultant in color photography to members of the trade. Naturally, his baby is his specialty—the dye

---

* Editors of Time-Life Books, *Color,* Life Library of Photography (New York: Time-Life Books, 1970), p. 68.

transfer. Speck says, "I have dyes hanging at home that I know have been on my wall since 1936, and they are very acceptable still today. So far, the aesthetic standard most people use is the dye transfer."

Guarantees Against Fading

Ken Lieberman, executive vice-president of the K&L Color Service, Inc. in New York City, states, "I have never had a dye transfer print returned to the lab because of fading." In business since 1949, K&L has a reputation for supporting the best efforts in color photography. With the opening of the K&L Gallery of Photographic Art in 1976, which is offering to corporations limited-edition color prints by well-known photographers, the company is including a fifty-year guarantee against fading for dye transfers, providing prints are hung under optimum conditions. What optimum conditions are seems to vary from authority to authority.

One of the problems basic to defining optimum conditions and determining print longevity is the fact that color processes used today have not been around long enough for conclusive scientific observation. Accelerated fade tests have been performed, but there is nothing like unequivocal evidence, especially when people must decide whether or not color photographs are a good investment, let alone a sensible buy.

Optimum Conditions for Color Prints

However, *absolute* optimum conditions will be hard for most collectors to provide. According to Lieberman, "A dye transfer shouldn't be subjected to direct ultraviolet rays of the sun. It shouldn't be hung where there are extreme temperature changes—for example, in a room kept air-conditioned cool by day and hot at night when the conditioner is off. A print shouldn't be exposed to intense ultraviolet rays from fluorescent lighting, either. By 'intense,' I mean higher wattage than one usually finds in an office. Fluorescent lights should have U.V. filters on them. I've had dyes on my office walls for ten years with no fading whatsoever. And high humidity is a no-no as well."

One begins to wonder what kind of environment can satisfy all these strictures. How are retirees in Florida going to cope, or expatriates in the Caribbean planning to decorate their homes with color photographs? What happens during the rainy season? Realizing the scope of the restrictions, Lieberman simply says, "Don't hang a dye in direct sunlight or under heavy fluorescent illumination and we will guarantee the life of the print for fifty years. If the color wanes, and we are reasonably convinced the print hasn't been hanging in someone's sun room for a few years, we'll replace it."

But by what process do they replace it? Frank McLaughlin, customer contact for the dye transfer devision at Kodak, says that the dye transfer process is "the only archival system of color photography that there is. It reduces a color transparency, or negative, to three silver separation negatives which are as stable as black and white negatives, providing they are properly cared for. These can be stored away and reprinted at any time. No other color system available today can make that statement."

This is true. The unfortunate fact of life is that original color materials —transparencies and negatives—fade under normal conditions, with visible damage in as short a time as twenty years. But dye transfer separation negatives are archivally permanent and can be kept on hand by either photographers themselves or the labs that pull their dyes. Therefore collectors may avail themselves of fresh prints when warranted.

Doubts about Guarantees

The guarantees offered by K&L Gallery of Photographic Art and by Photo Art Original, which is also issuing limited-edition color prints from Guadalajara, Mexico, carry with them some questions. In theory, responsible photographers should oversee the pulling of their own dye transfer prints. What happens if they're no longer in the land of the living when a collector feels justified in taking up a gallery on a guarantee? The collector may get a bright new print, but it will not be a "vintage" one. Neither will it be signed, a practice that color photographers are beginning to insist on. A gallery could also go bankrupt. What becomes of

DON WORTH (1924–   ). *Paul,* White Sands, New Mexico, 1974 (Collection of the artist).

Every magazine is a marketplace of images for the collector. Worth's *Paul* was first seen by the authors in a photography publication.

---

guarantees under this condition? Collectors are advised to buy from sound, reputable galleries! With the color market not yet firmly established, new galleries specializing in the medium may come and go.

In effect, the guarantees become a goodwill gesture. It is hoped they will remain just that. As Lieberman says, "We'll have the separation negatives on file. We may even be taken advantage of, but I'm so hopped up by people who refuse to buy color because it's going to fade that I'm doing all I can to help out."

Color Coupler versus Dye Transfer

The K&L gallery is also offering a twenty-five-year guarantee for what have generically become known as C prints but are properly termed color coupler prints. This betrays less faith in the stability of the color couplers than in the dyes. This position is supported by Robert Speck, the dye transfer expert, who says, "Technicians will try to tell me that other processes are just as stable as the dyes and they show me test fade figures, stating that the cyan has faded this much, the yellow this much, and the magenta this much. They say, 'Look. The total of what this paper fades is less than the total of what the dye transfer fades.' But here's the trick. When a dye fades, it loses yellow. If yellow goes by as much as 50 percent, your eye isn't affected by it. Let magenta or cyan fade 5 percent and it'll drive you crazy. When a color coupler goes, it loses magenta first. And that's the most murderous one. The question is: How does fading affect the eye after thirty to forty years? You have to look at *what* fades and *how much,* rather than at overall, general figures."

However, two specialists in color, working independently, agree on the answer to the question: If you hung a dye transfer print and a color coupler print in the same room, under the same conditions, which would fade faster? Dorothea Kehaya, master color printer, and Henry Wilhelm, author of *Preservation of Contemporary Photographic Materials,* concur that it would depend entirely on prevailing environmental conditions. Given the fact that heat, humidity, fluorescent light, direct sunlight, and air pollution levels are all the natural enemies of both print types, Kehaya and Wilhelm agree that each would react differently, at varying fade rates, according to the proportions of the deleterious elements in the environment. In other words, one process may have a lower tolerance for humidity, which may be the dominant factor in the room. Another may have more resistance to fluorescent lighting, and so on. The upshot of their response is that a collector would have to hire someone to come into his or her home and evaluate the conditions before prescribing a print type. One can hardly see this becoming regular practice for the average collector.

Cibachrome, the Newcomer

A newcomer in the color photographic print arena is Cibachrome, a process of the Ciba-Geigy Corp. Its initial intention was to capture the wedding and portrait market. But the high stability of the Cibachrome print has the art photography world flirting with it as a third alternative for collecting color. Says Speck, "Its my guess that Ciba-Geigy has chosen the highest-stability azo dyes for their Cibachrome process. It's likely that Cibas are what they're claimed to be—very stable. Their technicians have the option to choose dyes with the greatest stability, whereas in dye transfer there are so many individual characteristics required that you just can't choose any cyan or any magenta. You have to use specific ones, and they may not be of the highest stability. On the other hand, you have to face the question of whether the Cibachrome process gives you a good reproduction. The contrast level is very high."

Speck raises one of the biggest drawbacks that Cibachrome has in appealing to art photographers. Its high contrast level makes it technically difficult to work with as a standard process.

Another property of the Cibachrome print that has not found universal acceptance is its super-glossy surface, a quality that enables it to capture the fullest range of colors. Some photographers and collectors respond to it as they might to satin sheets. Other people like shine, whether it's on their shoes or on photographic prints. It's a matter of personal taste. There are sprays available as an antidote, but they flatten out the three-dimensional quality uniquely native to the Cibachrome print.

It is hoped that Ciba-Geigy can square away some of these drawbacks so that collectors can take advantage of Cibachrome's high stability level. Stan Clay, manager of technical services for the company, confirms that it is making regular progress in overcoming the limitations. In fact, there is talk already of advances to be announced in the next year or so.

Kodak also continues to address itself to the stability issue. Frank McLaughlin says, "Yes, dye transfer prints and color coupler prints have been improved over the years. Are they archivally permanent? The answer is, frankly, 'No.' Of course, we're cognizant of the fact that it'd be

BERNHARDT and HILLA BECHER (1931–   and 1934–   ). *Typography of Framework Houses,* ca. 1974 (Sonnabend Gallery).

Devoted to showing all sides of a subject, the Bechers meticulously record homes, factories, and construction sites throughout Europe. As "Conceptualist" photographers, the husband-and-wife team are forerunners.

desirable to have an indelible color print. Kodak continues to research and come up with new compounds as it has over the last forty years."

Other Color Media Fade, Too

What is a collector to think about the stability problem? It may or may not be comforting to realize that color work in most media fades in the long run. One should take this into consideration when buying a water-color, a lithograph, an oil, *or* a photograph. Nonetheless, the difference

---

PAUL CAPONIGRO (1932–   ). *Sunflower,* 1965 (Collection of the artist).
Caponigro's passionate approach to nature photography is evidenced by the variety of images he has made of so simple a subject as the sunflower.

between color photography and the others is the fact that major museums and institutions have had the time and taken the money to develop intelligent restoration and preservation systems for older media. Certainly, Japanese wood block prints, for example, must be conserved with utmost delicacy. Affirms a photographer, "Color photographs aren't unique in art history for their lack of stone carving quality of archival permanence."

International Museum of Photography Takes the Lead

A few institutions are beginning to take steps to preserve color photographic prints in the most responsible ways known to date, including the International Museum of Photography at George Eastman House. William Jenkins, assistant curator at the International Museum, says, "We weren't convinced it was wise to collect color, and now we are. We're beginning to build cold storage facilities for our color collection, starting with small refrigeration units. As the collection grows, we'll have to get bigger ones. We will take out what we want to exhibit, and return the prints to cold storage when shows are taken down. We wanted very badly to collect color, but we didn't know if it was responsible or not. The turning point in our decision was the Color Colloquium at George Eastman House last year. The dye-stability experts at Kodak have done accelerated aging tests and came up with some reassuring conclusions. Now, I'm not holding up Eastman Kodak's engineers as being the last word on the subject, but we have to listen to somebody. They felt that the right materials, processed correctly, and kept sufficiently cold and dry, could meet archival standards, which in our terms is three hundred years, with no measurable change. We figured, if they say so, we'll try it!"

Needless to say, the International Museum at George Eastman House is in fine financial condition to install the necessary costly facilities to meet their high archival standards. But most other institutions and private collectors are not.

Which print type is the International Museum collecting? Says Jenkins, "Despite the arguments that color coupler prints are as stable as dyes, the dye stability experts at Eastman Kodak who attended our Color Colloquium are convinced that the dye transfer is considerably more stable. However, we collect color coupler prints as well. It's just that you have to keep them cold and dry. Optimum conditions are forty degrees and 40 percent humidity—colder than air conditioning. But if one wanted to hang a color coupler print on one's living room wall with no ultraviolet light around, and no ultraviolet light–absorbing Plexiglas over the photograph, in relatively low humidity, they will last a very long time. You shouldn't be able to measure any fading, either visually or with instruments, for at least ten years.

"But when we are talking about museum collecting, we're not talking about a useful life for something decorative on your wall. We're talking about preserving the thing for future generations.

"Another reason we collect C prints is because dyes are so terribly expensive. Also, take photographers like Neal Slavin or Stephen Shore. They don't like the way their pictures look in dye transfer. The point is that well-processed color coupler prints are stable enough to collect. Any collector should find out whether or not the print he's buying was processed by a decent, technically responsible color lab. It can be tricky with photographers who make their own C prints. You don't know what their quality controls are, although they could very well be higher than in a commercial lab. Somebody who is serious about developing an ongoing collection of color wouldn't be too nuts to buy a $400 refrigerator."

Cold Storage?

Henry Wilhelm, author of *Preservation of Contemporary Photographic Materials,* agrees. "But don't run out and buy any icebox at the nearest Sears, Roebuck," he says. "You need a low-humidity refrigerator." Wilhelm, who has been doing deep research into all problems relative to fading and the preservation of color, has written perhaps the most definitive book on the subject, one for which the photographic community has waited for years. In it he prescribes refrigeration units best suited for color materials.

"Humbug" is the way some people respond, including Frank McLaughlin at Kodak. "I can see photographers taking Wilhelm's advice and keeping their negatives and transparencies in refrigerators. This isn't a new idea. But what's the use of storing prints in refrigerators? You can't look at them. I'd hang them on a wall instead."

Most Collectable Print Type?

Refrigeration notwithstanding, what does it all boil down to? What print type should collectors buy? There are, indeed, some photographers who will allow their work to be reproduced only in dye transfer form, firmly believing it to be the best of all possible worlds. Color rendition can be more accurately controlled in the dye process, and it's the only one whereby the photographers' originals can be reduced to archivally permanent separation negatives. Naturally, what the collector can afford is going to be a primary determining factor. At this point, the Cibachromes are the least expensive; the color couplers slightly more; and, the dyes . . . they cost! This is because dye transfer is the most complicated process technically, requiring more steps, and more man hours.

From a quality point of view, all three processes are considered acceptable, given their individual characteristics. Ed Scully, consulting editor to *Modern Photography* magazine, conducted an interesting test for the Society for Photographic Education. He had a dye transfer, a color coupler, and a Cibachrome print made of one of his 35 mm Kodachrome transparencies of the camel souk at Goulimine, Morocco. Scully concluded: "It was obvious that there were large differences in the appearance of the prints. Not only in those variables that you can control in printing, but in the very nature of each process and the way each produced its contrasts and colors. But no one could really say that one print was 'better' than the other. . . ." *

Collectors should become at least visually familiar with each process, taking into consideration that most photographers have definite ideas about the print process that most becomes their work. It would be very

* Scully, Ed, "Color," *Modern Photography* (July, 1976), p. 70.

doubtful if William Eggleston would allow his "none-color" color photographs to be made up in shiny Cibachrome, for example.

Criteria for Collecting Color

Still, the average collector is in a quandary as to the collectability of color photographs. There are so many ifs, ands, or buts surrounding the medium. The matter seems best boiled down to: if you want to collect color as a decorative item, select the print type that appeals to you, that you can afford, or that the photographer dictates. Hang the prints with as much attention as you can give to the optimum conditions defined in this chapter. Your photographs will most likely grow old gracefully with you. And think of it, your prints are guaranteed against fading if purchased through certain galleries. You are not guaranteed against fading! The prints may very well outlive you, and in very acceptable condition. Your color photographs will have been an investment in pleasure for your lifetime.

If, however, you intend to pass down your collection from generation to generation with the notion that your investment might be of benefit to heirs, or if it is a corporate collection being passed from one board of directors to another, you'd best consider darkness and refrigeration along with the optimum conditions prescribed for the times you wish to have your prints on display. As for museums that collect, or wish to collect, color, they will want to be as responsible as finances allow.

A prominent authority on the preservation and restoration of photographic collections and curator of photography at the Smithsonian Institution, Eugene Ostroff, says, "Collecting color photographs is a compromise." It seems to be, pending future technological breakthroughs in archival permanence for color prints.

Aesthetic Doubts about Color

Color photography faces another question that is as much of a thorn in its side as the stability issue. There are some who do not feel that color

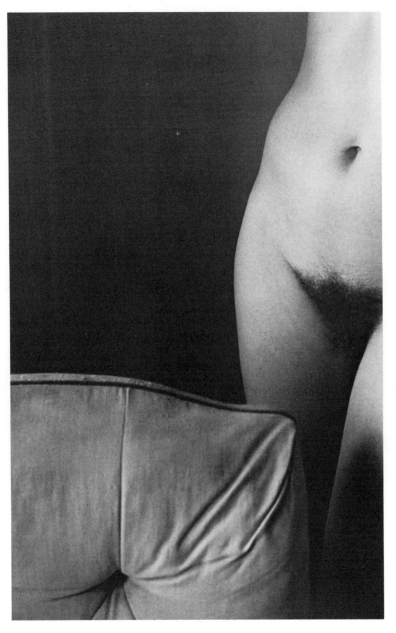

EVA RUBINSTEIN (1934–   ). *Nude with Chair,* 1975 (Neikrug Gallery).
Humor and classicism combine in this strong, sensuous graphic photograph.
A prime example of the escalating price of photographs, Rubinstein's portfolio
was $475 in 1974. Now it is $750. Soon it will be $1,000.

JERRY UELSMANN (1934–   ). Untitled, 1969 (Collection of the artist).
   Uelsmann's photomontages are printed individually by exposing paper to more than one negative, or by exposing paper to a sandwich of more than one negative. He also uses semi-transparent objects, including leaves, as negatives.

is a viable medium for serious expression in photography. Those contemplating color for their collections should be familiar with the reasons.

First of all, there has been little evidence to suggest that color should be taken seriously. Few color photographers have produced remarkable bodies of work compared to the many black and white photographers who have. The painter-writer-photographer Syl Labrot said, "I've seen many photographs with very beautiful color situations that would stand up favorably to modern art. The problem is that these are isolated. They are not driven through as an aesthetic. I don't think color photographers have confronted the aesthetic challenges of the medium at all."

Labrot goes on to say, however, that "there has been very little solid support for people working in color. Even today, there is little dialogue about it, little exhibited, and little is reproduced compared to black and white. Photography flourishes through the reproductive media: books, magazines, catalogs, etc. The photography magazines publish color, but they aren't what I'm talking about. Serious creative magazines, like *Aperture, Artforum,* and *Photograph,* don't have the money to reproduce much color. So it isn't simply that there aren't enough important bodies of work around. The two go hand in hand. With no encouragement, photographers seek other directions."

This dilemma is confirmed by the fact that a major graphics collectors' club, beginning to offer black and white photographs to its members, won't consider color. One of the reasons is that the club could not even afford color brochures on a regular basis.

But still, it is hard to think of many photographers who have dealt with the medium successfully, integrating color, form, and content with equal strength. John Szarkowski, who organized the Eggleston show at the Museum of Modern Art in 1976, writes in the show's catalog that the failures of color "might be divided into two categories. The more interesting of these might be described as black-and-white photographs made with color film, in which the problem of color is solved by inattention. The better photographs of the old *National Geographic* were often of this sort: no matter how cobalt the blue skies and how crimson the red shirts, the color in such pictures is extraneous—a failure of form."

Indeed, photographers working for *National Geographic* are advised to forget that they have color film in their cameras, and shoot only for content.

Szarkowski continues: "The second category of failure in color photography comprises photographs of beautiful colors in pleasing relationships. The nominal subject matter of these pictures is often the walls of old buildings, or the prows of sailboats reflected in rippled water. Such photographs can be recognized by their resemblance to reproductions of Synthetic Cubist or Abstract Expressionist paintings. It is their unhappy fate to remind us of something similar but better. . . . Most color photography, in short, has been either formless or pretty."

This latter viewpoint is difficult to accept as a blanket criticism. Yes, there are many too many photographs of old walls, torn posters, graffiti, and so on, but there are as many of this type of subject matter in black and white as there are in color! Does Aaron Siskind succeed with *Homage to Franz Kline,* abstract brushstrokes on stucco, because it is monochromatic, while Ernst Haas fails with *Bird Taking Off,* a black and red abstraction of a torn poster, simply because it is in color? Is the subject matter of one more "nominal" than the other?

An automatic assumption that Haas's color image is more "nominal" is based on the fact that most color photography has been merely decorative in the past. The reason again is that few workers in the medium have successfully juggled form, content, and color. Most work in the medium has ridden on color primarily; form, secondarily; and content, seldom. Color photographers will have a hard time living this down. They are juggling three factors, not just two, as in black and white. Color photography is a more challenging medium than meets the eye. And collectors will want to be on the alert for successful color work.

The plain truth is, it is high time that photographers take the color issue to task, conceptually. A. D. Coleman said, "As a critic, the thing that bothers me about color photographers is that most of them are committed to making beautiful images, rather than powerful, perhaps even ugly images. Consequently, those beautiful images pall for me. They are simply beautiful color combinations with perhaps some form. They are too often decoration. For me, color will have come of age when color is used, but where the attractiveness, what Duchamp called a 'retinal response,' is not the overriding response."

Marie Cosindas, the John Singer Sargent of Polaroid portraiture, and a forerunner of today's color movement, has for more than a decade avoided color for color's sake. Her low-key, painterly hues, achieved by completely controlling the subject, the clothes worn, the surroundings, lighting, and so forth, have given her work a sophistication lacking in other modes of color photography. The "retinal response" to her portraits is not touched off by color alone.

On the other hand, if some color photography is beautiful and decorative, it seems a shame that the photographic community, as well as collectors, cannot accept it on this basis. The insistence that beauty, in and of itself, is insubstantial in the color medium may be sadly reflective of a society for which ugliness, urban blight, and psychological turmoil are the prevailing realities. Certainly these tensions are being explored extensively by black and white photographers. Unfortunately, beauty doesn't seem to hold its own, in the eyes of many photography critics.

New Schools of Color Photography

Paul Outerbridge, a successful advertising photographer working in color in the 1930s and '40s, said: "One very important difference between color and monochromatic photography is this: in black and white you suggest; in color you state. Much can be implied by suggestion, but statement demands certainty . . . absolute certainty." *

Outerbridge would find that today "certainty" and "idea" are just beginning to enter the color medium. In the past, few photographers have defined the problems of color and deliberately set out to solve them, as painters have done for decades. Stepping forward to meet the challenge, and of special appeal to current collectors, is a school of Conceptualist color photographers, considered by some to be antiphotography photographers. These people eschew the technical, and simply use the medium to solve a problem, just as Muybridge utilized photography for his

* Scully, Julia, "Seeing Pictures," *Modern Photography* (Oct., 1976), p. 8.

Esta caused a Commotion at mass,
By wearing a hat on her ass.
And she found that it stayed,
Even when she got laid,
Now you've got to admit, that's class

DUANE MICHALS (1936–   ). *Esta Limerick,* 1974 (Sidney Janis Gallery).
    "Nice photographs are not enough," says Michals. Indeed, many of his images and sequences are not nice nor as amusing as Esta. But they demand the active rather than passive attention of the viewer. Given to innovation, Michals often clarifies the psychological message of his images by handwritten statements on the borders of his prints.

Animal Locomotion studies. Among these artists are Jan Groover, John Baldessari, Jan Dibbets, and William Wegman. They work in color, not for color's sake, but because the depth and dimension that color achieves are essential to their idea. Some of these people don't even want to be called photographers, in fact.

Ralph Gibson, as well, an established photographer in black and white, has taken up an aesthetic problem in color and is working with it. Gibson's career began in the Navy with aerial and applied photography. He has been a photojournalist and has done fashion, advertising, and annual report assignments. For the last ten years he has been an "art photographer," as we know him today. This experience spans twenty years. Only now as an art photographer is Gibson turning to color as a natural next step.

Gibson's example of a progressing career points out a possible pitfall in color photography. Younger workers in the medium have undergone few of the disciplines of making successful images of varying intent in black and white, and some would rather avoid the darkroom altogether. There are those who feel that basic to successful color imagery is an ability to deal with form and content in monochrome. Without this background, the work of some color photographers tends to be glib.

Another realm where the color medium is beginning to find expanding expression is in non-straight photographic processes. Some people believe that direct color photography is limiting in that one cannot edit out distracting color elements in a photograph. This growing band includes Gail Skoff, Karen Truax, and Suzanne Seed, all of whom selectively hand-color black and white images to overcome this problem.

A. D. Coleman says, "For me, among the most interesting color photographs have been those which are really 'colored images' rather than straight photographs." By this he is referring to those contemporary pictures which are the result of a resurgence of an old process. Hand-tinted daguerreotype portraits were the rage from practically the beginning of the photographic medium. But interesting new work with hand-applied dyes is being done.

Karen Truax says: "My reasons for applying color to my photographs go far beyond any desire to duplicate reality: if it were, I would use a true color process. I do use colors that allude to reality. My purpose in applying color to an object is not to change it—as in painting a rock pink or skin purple—but rather I am concerned with the emotional effects and the symbolic implications of color. Therefore, the colors I select and the extent to which I use them on my photographs becomes very intentional. Since I apply color by hand, I have a choice as to whether or not I want to color all or only part of the photograph. Hand coloring gives me the greatest sense of personal satisfaction. My moment of greatest joy is to watch the print evolve to where I previsioned it." *

Another growing movement under the color banner of interest to collectors is what one might call hybrid photography—the cross-fertilization of photographic processes with the graphic arts, of which Robert Heinecken and Syl Labrot are preeminent practitioners. This marriage, largely the result of the proximity of photographic and graphic arts in the educational system, has met with a mixed reception by the Establishment. There are some who do not feel that incorporating photographs in silk screen processes, photographic collages, and the like qualifies as legitimate photography. However, others feel that these artists are moving photography into broader dimensions and expanding existing definitions of the medium.

Technical Doubts about Color

Apart from these aesthetic tensions over color photography, there is yet another technical doubt as to the medium's viability for serious artistic expression. What the eye sees and what color films and processes are capable of recording are two different things. The black and white photographer can previsualize his finished prints much more easily than can the color photographer. Color emulsions change, familiar films are phased out by manufacturers, quality controls in custom labs fluctuate. And the nature of the beast seems to take the making of the finished print

* Truax, Karen, "Colors of My Hand," *Camera 35* (May, 1976), p. 49.

GEORGE TICE (1938–   ). *Pitchfork,* Lancaster, Pa., 1968 (Collection of the artist).

Many contemporary photographers dislike the darkroom. However, Tice is an exception and has made a name for himself as a master printer. Quality prints are important to collectors.

out of the hands of the creator, losing that personal touch. There is, however, a drift toward making their own C prints by photographers including Dorothea Kehaya and Neal Slavin.

Syl Labrot, in fact, feels, "I think anyone doing anything with color will have to work in the medium themselves. They cannot have other people process their prints. The only way you can get away with it is if you are going to use color in an offhand sense, as does Eggleston, the bland photorealist. Eggleston uses color incidentally. His are basically good black and white pictures. These a lab can do satisfactorily. Color is a real hassle to do yourself, but photographers are going to have to if 'color,' as such, is important to their work."

The inability of photographers to control with exactness the colors of a print has been a major criticism of the medium. The modern artist gets away with any color combinations—bilious greens and arresting reds—because he can mix them to his own taste. In photography it would be assumed that these shades were neither reality, nor intentional, but the result of technical limitations—"miscolor."

Beaumont Newhall writes in the *History of Photography* that "the line between the photographer and the painter is no more clearly drawn than in color photography. Imitation is fatal. By the nature of his medium, the photographer's vision must be rooted in reality; if he attempts to create his own world of color, he faces a double dilemma: his results no longer have that unique quality we can only define as 'photographic,' and he quickly discovers that with only three primary colors, modulated in intensity by three emulsions obeying sensitometric laws, he cannot hope to rival the painter with the range of pigments which he can place at will upon the canvas. On the other hand, the painter cannot hope to rival the accuracy, detail, and, above all the authenticity of the photographs." *

This being the case, the color photographic medium should be accepted for its limitations and assets just as painting has been. "My feel-

* Newhall, Beaumont, *The History of Photography* (New York: The Museum of Modern Art, 1964), p. 194.

DEBORAH TURBEVILLE (1938–   ). *Black and White Bath House,* 1975 (Collection of the artist).

A trend setter in fashion photography, Turbeville startles and intrigues the public. Her unique approach to commercial photography is now sought after by private collectors as well.

---

ing is that the end product, the photograph, is something in itself. It doesn't have to look like anything," says Stephen Shore.

Indeed, monochrome is very far removed from the colored reality of the world around us. Why insist that the color medium necessarily be realistically accurate, providing the artist approves of the final print? But some people simply cannot stop worrying at the issue. A. D. Coleman feels that the work being done by Lucas Samaras and Les Krims with the Polaroid SX-70 is more legitimate than C prints or dye transfers because "the color of the SX-70 is inevitable. It's a 'given' for the photographer. It probably sounds silly, but this helps me accept the SX-70 a great deal more."

To photographers such as Pete Turner, Art Kane, and Jay Maisel, it probably does sound "silly." They, among others, assiduously administer the pulling of their outsized dye transfer prints, often rejecting five or six before one meets their color standards. It would be financially unrealistic for these artists to install their own labs, although there may come a time when photo artists will have cooperative color labs where quality controls can be carefully monitored, and where they don't have to compete with the everyday traffic of large commercial operations.

But at this point it would be hard for collectors to insist that prints be made by the photographers themselves. In fact, those photographers who do oversee commercial laboratory technicians follow in the tradition of an artist in attendance at an "imprimerie" when a print-maker pulls his prints. Such work is done under the "supervision" of the artist or artist-photographer.

All ifs, ands, or buts aside, the future looks brighter for color photography. It cannot be denied that because more color is being shown at the Museum of Modern Art, dealers, collectors, and other museums will be paying greater attention to the medium. This will, we hope, stimulate long-overdue solid support of color photography. With this encouragement, we will no doubt see effective new color work surface in the time to come, and credit given to deserving artists who have been working in color for many years.

Color photography may well become an exciting new frontier for collectors on all levels.

7 | Photography Prices Today and Tomorrow

WHAT THE COLLECTOR AND THE INVESTOR NEED TO KNOW

"I have no difficulty accepting the fact that some people collect photographs for investment purposes. Photographers who are upset about commercialism in the galleries sound as if they don't want anybody to hear their music. Chartres is a beautiful cathedral, despite the fact that the workmen were paid."

—HARRY CALLAHAN

IN THE EARLY 1930S THE METROPOLITAN MUSEUM BOUGHT 600 Mathew Brady photographs for ten cents apiece. Each one is worth a minimum of $1,000 today. About the same time, one of the museum's staff members was going to England. As an afterthought, he was given $150 to buy some Julia Margaret Camerons. He did—150 of them. In 1976 few of the great lady's images were available for less than $1,200 each.

Cameron Album Sold for $120,000

In fact, in 1974 collector Sam Wagstaff paid $120,000 at Sotheby's Belgravia for an album containing ninety-four photographs presented by Mrs. Cameron to Sir John Herschel, the noted scientist. The thought of such a national treasure leaving its homeland was sufficiently shattering that the British Reviewing Committee on the Export of Works of Art withheld an export license. It was the first time this had ever happened in Great Britain to anything photographic.

Public donations, together with an appropriation from the National Art-Collection Fund, saved the album and it is now safely housed at the National Portrait Gallery in London. Ironically enough, only a short time

171

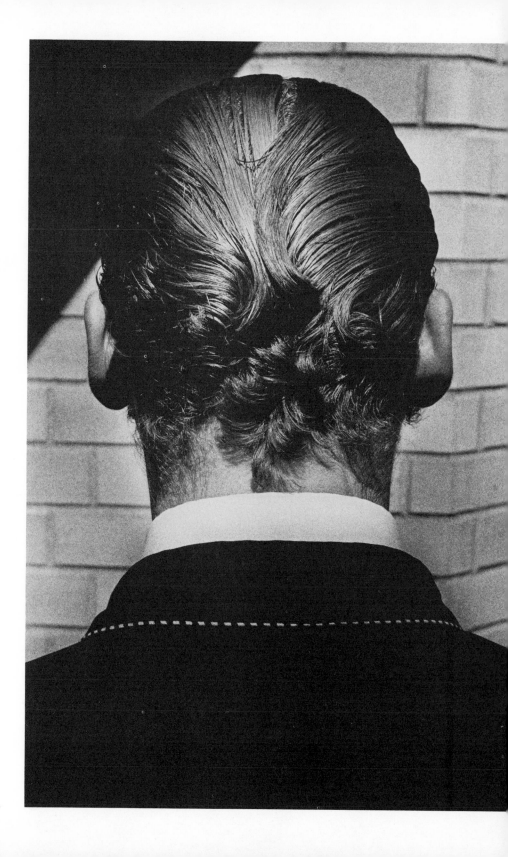

previously the gallery had also acquired, for $80,000, some 258 Hill and Adamson photographs that had been a part of the Royal Academy and that no one had asked to see in over one hundred years.

Today photographs are steadily increasing in popularity and therefore in price. Because, as has been explained, photographic prints are nowhere near as numerous as the general public would believe, savvy collectors have zeroed in on the truth and competition for certain photographers' key images has accelerated, with astonishing results.

Take, for example, the man who bought six daguerreotypes for $20 in San Francisco several years ago. When these were authenticated by the Library of Congress as originals by John Plumbe taken in 1846, the new owner turned around and sold them for $12,000. Or there is the case of the daguerreotype portrait of President Martin Van Buren, circa 1856, bought for $45 in a Pennsylvania antique shop, then resold for $6,000 shortly afterward. And there is the much-publicized tale of the 1848 daguerreotype by an unknown photographer of Edgar Allan Poe. It sold for $9,250 at a Chicago auction in 1973, was resold immediately for a reputed $18,000 to New York dealer Scott Elliot, and subsequently purchased by collector Arnold Crane for over $35,000!

The Poe tale is a good example not only of the profits to be made by dealers but of the passion and expense expended by some photography lovers to get what they want.

Set of *Camera Works* Sold for $35,700

But it was those who bought photographs twenty years or more ago who did extraordinarily well. Consider the purchaser of 1,100 prints by Eadweard Muybridge of his great work *Animal Locomotion,* which sold for $250 in 1952 at New York's Swann Auction Gallery. They are worth

---

RALPH GIBSON (1939–   ). *Doorman,* Park Ave., 1975 (Castelli Graphics).
A guru of the photography workshop circuit, Gibson has moved progressively closer to his subjects. The photographs in his Quadrants series are mainly details of people's faces and clothing.

at least $165,000 on today's market. Or the person who bought three copies of *Camera Works,* with its many photogravures, for $11, sometimes worth over $5,000 apiece today. The publication originally cost $8 a year for a subscription; the heirs of those who saved their fifty issues can do astonishingly well. In May, 1975, Sotheby Parke Bernet auctioned a set, volume by volume, for $35,750.

Even more startling now is the price paid at the 1952 Swann sale for Fox Talbot's *The Pencil of Nature.* For $200, someone landed the photographically illustrated book, considered the Gutenberg Bible of photography by many. It would probably bring $50,000 on the market in 1977 —that is, if one were even to become available.

In the 1950s Lucien Goldschmidt also made history by selling 350 Atget prints for $1 apiece. They are worth at least $1,500 individually at this time.

Contemporary Photographers' Works Rise in Price

As the photo boom surges ahead, it should be noted that the high prices are not only for the most sought-after nineteenth-century vintage material. Certain twentieth-century photographers, both still alive and recently deceased, are climbing higher, too. For instance, Ansel Adams's prints went from $350 in June, 1974, to $500 in September, 1975. After he announced in January, 1976, that he will do no more personalized printing after he is through his current back orders, Adams's photographs now fetch a minimum of $800 a print. An old platinum print by Imogen Cunningham that sold for $500 in 1974 rose to $1,500 in 1975. Berenice Abbott prints were about $100 in 1969. They average $400 or more now. Eugene Smith's *Madness* recently fetched $750, roughly 200 percent more than it did twelve months before. "It's enough to drive even Smith to the darkroom," quips Jacqueline Brody, editor of *The Print Collector's Newsletter.* Black and white prints by George Tice are up from about $25 in 1970 to around $175; Eliot Porter, from $100 to $250; Harry Callahan, from $150 to as much as $450; and Wynn Bullock, from $100 to around $250.

Where these photographers' prices will be six months from now, no one knows. It is one of the reasons that publications hesitate to quote photography prices today. But one thing is certain. With death comes almost instantaneous reevaluation of an artist's work and a subsequent shift upward in the prices for their images. Take Diane Arbus. She was fortunate to get $150 a print when she was alive. A check for $1,500 isn't unusual for a collector to write for one of her photographs now that she's gone. The day after Walker Evans passed on, his portfolio rose from $3,500 to $5,000, according to *Museum News*.

"God knows what is going to happen to their prices when we lose Abbott, Kertész, Brassaï, Adams, and other great masters who are still alive, but who are, to be honest, senior citizens today. This is the end of a great era on photography," a dealer confides. "It may also be the day of five-and-ten-cent store prices for great contemporary photographers' works. It's sad to say, but it's often after someone has gone that the market really takes off."

It should be pointed out, though, that up isn't the only direction for photo prices to go. Tastes fluctuate, and prices can do the same. For instance, Rejlander's albumen print *The Head of John the Baptist in a Charger* fell recently at an auction to $850, one third of its price two years ago. Also F. H. Evans's *Portrait of Aubrey Beardsley* sold for only $500, almost half its price in 1974. At the same time, though, a Paul Outerbridge doubled to $1,000 in one year.

Established Names, the Safest Investment

While there is no stabilization of prices yet in the photography marketplace, it is true that established names in photography are the safest bet. "Nobody wants the unknown," says Alice Adams of Chicago's Frumkin Gallery. "They want names. That's the game." Therefore, anyone who wants to have a photography hedge fund will go down the indexes in the Gernsheims' and Newhall's histories and say, "I'll take one of his, one of hers, two of his, three of hers," and let their collecting go at that. Boring, yes. But a pretty sure approach to photography as an investment. A bit like buying only Rodins, or El Grecos, or Calders.

Remember, though, in photography collecting "the most sought-after prints are those that were printed and signed by a noted photographer at the time the negative was made. Photos printed and signed later by the photographer are next. Then come prints that the photographer made but didn't sign, followed by prints made by someone else and signed by the photographer," according to *Business Week* (and reputable dealers). "An unsigned print made after the photographer's death by a noted craftsman has value, too—but considerably less. A photo signed and printed by the late Edward Weston, for example, is worth up to $3,000. A print made by his son Cole—even though it is from the same Edward Weston negative—can only bring $150 to $200. Connoisseurs can tell the difference." *

The Value of Vintage Prints

Collector Arnold Crane is even more outspoken when he cautions collectors who are interested in photographs for love and profit. Stressing the value of vintage prints, those made by the photographer himself close to the time when he took the image, Crane insists that collectors should "run, don't walk, from anything but vintage work, for the vintage work has the unexplained magic of presence; that actual presence of the master creator. Avoid at any cost those posthumous 'limited editions,' those Edward Weston prints made by his sons under his direction. And those Walker Evans portfolios printed by one of his students and Frederick H. Evans portfolios printed by one of his disciples. Avoid all posthumous printing as one would avoid a posthumous restrike from a Daumier stone.

* "Personal Business," *Business Week* (Oct. 20, 1975), p. 105.

KIPTON KUMLER (1940–   ). *New Brunswick,* 1972 (Schoelkopf Gallery).
While many photographers support their art by teaching, Kumler is on the staff of The Arthur D. Little Co. in Cambridge, Mass. His classical photographs of plant life and architecture are taken during off-hours.

They are unimportant in their essence and are useful only as classroom reference material—or for fireplace tinder." *

Strong words, but understandable when put beside Aaron Siskind's reply to a question posed to him by Harold Jones, director of Tucson's Center for Creative Photography. Asked if he didn't think that a print made by him had more meaning than one made by someone else, Siskind at first replied in the negative. Then, he thought again. "I wasn't stating my case altogether honestly," he reconsidered. "Because when I tell you that this guy's print [of my negative] is as good as mine, that's true. But *if* I took that negative and I *was interested* in reprinting it, I don't know what I'd come out with. I'd come out with something else, because that would be another act, you see." †

It is precisely this mystique, this intangible, personal input that any artist transmits to his or her work, that causes truly professional collectors to go after the work taken by, printed by, and, it is to be hoped, signed by the photographer himself. For financial and for aesthetic reasons.

"Not only the attitude toward the subjects, but also the printing differs from artist to artist—the glistening image, the texture of the paper or the gradations of black are all distinguishing and important aspects," adds Manuela Hoelterhoff in *The Wall Street Journal*. "For example, there is the expert darkroom manipulations of Jerry Uelsmann who utilizes several negatives for a single final print that is every bit as fascinating as a collage by Robert Rauschenberg." ‡

One of the reasons that portfolios—printed, signed, and numbered by photographers—are expected to become more prevalent is this very insistence by more collectors on having photographs produced "from start to finish" by their originators. Berenice Abbott, W. Eugene Smith, and Laura Gilpin are now working on their portfolios. Other photographers,

---

* Crane, Arnold, "Advice from a Photography Collector," *The New York Times* (Oct. 12, 1975), sect. 2, p. 31.

† Photographers & Professionals: A Discussion," *The Print Collector's Newsletter,* vol. 4, no. 3 (July/August, 1973), p. 60.

‡ Hoelterhoff, Manuela, "Why the Photography Market is Booming," *The Wall Street Journal* (Oct. 8, 1975).

including Lee Friedlander, Harry Callahan, Manuel Alvarez Bravo, Lartigue, Elliott Erwitt, Judy Dater, and Arnold Newman have already done so. The fame of the photographer, the size of the edition, the number of prints in it, the profit demands of the artist and his publisher: all these factors play a part in the pricing of a portfolio, most of which sell for between $1,200 and $3,000 at this time. But again—check on who did the printing, just as you would with an individual print. Portfolios printed "under the supervision of . . ." may very well *not* increase in value as much as those that have been personally printed. And with the proliferation of portfolios, the chances are there will be a greater number processed in commercial laboratories.

Portfolios Can Be a Good Investment

For the fast-moving collector-investor who gets in early, a portfolio can be a remarkably good investment, though. For instance, the Neikrug Gallery, which published Eva Rubinstein's portfolio of twelve prints in an edition of thirty-five, put a $475 price tag on it. Two months later it was up to $575, and by April, 1976, when there were ten portfolios left, the gallery raised the Rubinstein portfolio to $750. "When you realize that individual prints from this portfolio, or any of the artist's work, sell for over $100 apiece, you can see how good a buy a portfolio can be," says Marge Neikrug.

Another example of the fast-rising prices of portfolios occurred in September, 1976. Issuing an edition of fifteen of Lilo Raymond's *Still Life* portfolio of five images at $550, Scott Elliot of Helios Gallery raised the figure to $750 twenty-four hours later. "We sold three of Lilo's portfolios today," he said at a crowded cocktail party the day the artist's work went on display. "If I don't raise the price, it's obvious that I won't have any of the portfolios left."

In short, it's a matter of supply and demand again. Other photographers realize this basic economic rule and prefer to publish their own portfolios and reap the profits. Paul Caponigro, for instance, doubled the price of his *Portfolio Two* to $1,600 in 1976, three years after he'd published it for $800.

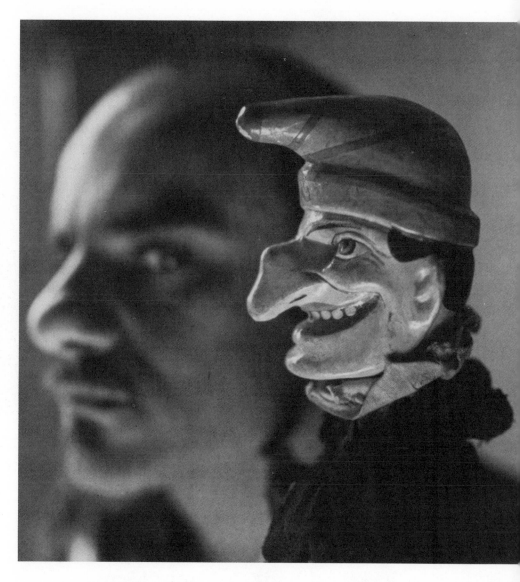

ARTHUR TRESS (1942–   ). *Charles Ludlum,* Punchman, 1975 (Collection of the artist).

Tress sees through the minds of his subjects and persuades them to do extraordinary things to carry out his perceptions. There is a bit of the grand guignol in his images.

MARK COHEN (1943–   ). Untitled, Wilkes-Barre, Pa., 1976 (Castelli Gallery).

The successful snapshot depends upon the quick perception and reflex of the photographer. This present-day technique is ideal for capturing a mood because the subjects are often unaware of the camera.

While the majority of portfolios go to museums and collectors who hold on to them, it is, of course, possible for speculators to buy them, break them up, and sell the images individually. This is what has happened to many graphic artists' limited editions and what may well happen more often with portfolios of photographs. At the present, though, photographically illustrated books may be the first to experience this sad but all too common marketing technique, according to Harry Lunn. "We're

LES KRIMS (1943–   ). *Uranium Robot,* 1976 (Light Gallery).

Krims, who teaches at Buffalo State University, held a robot construction contest, open to the entire student body. He then made a series of amusing yet sophisticated photographs of the forms that resulted.

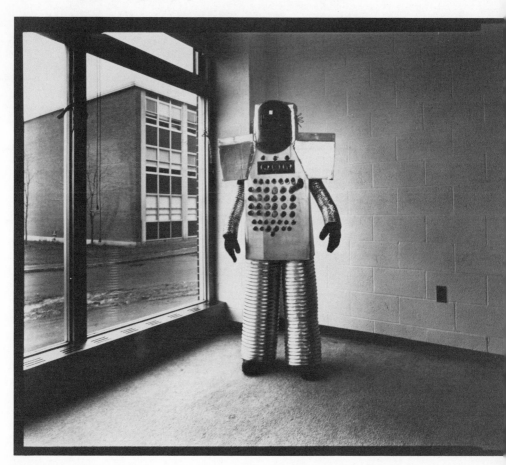

reaching the point with Gardner's *Photographic Sketch Book of the* [Civil] *War* which print dealers reached with Picasso's 'Suite Vollard,' " he says. "It is no longer interesting to sell the Suite as a complete unit. But you go back ten years and you could buy it for $14,000. The last time one sold, it went for about $250,000. So it came to the point where dealers started to split them up. Initially, they sold them in pairs. The two best prints, #27 and #97, were sold as a sort of package deal. I think you're going to see the same thing happen with the *Sketch Book.* The images are going to be broken up and sold individually." *

A good deal of the basis for Lunn's remarks is due to the fact that the famous *Sketch Book* with 100 mounted pictures can go for as much as $20,000 today, up from $1,000 in 1967. With only an estimated 200 copies ever published, and virtually impossible to buy, dealer expectation is for continued escalation of price.

Collectors Look for Books Containing Rare Photographs

Still, when rare books with photographs do come on the market, the price per image continues to be remarkably reasonable. Citing as an example Thomas Annan's (1829–1887) *The Streets of Glasgow,* which fetched $10,000 at a recent sale, Lunn says, "When you glance down the records of the same auction and see the most mundane, almost obnoxious Chagall selling for $2,500 in an edition of 100, I don't think $250 an image for an Annan is excessive." †

Neither, apparently, did the purchaser. Or the person who bought an album of sixteen photographs published in Edinburgh in 1867 entitled *Antiquities in Cambodia.* Admittedly this was a rare album; nevertheless the auction house estimated it would sell for between $1,000 and $2,000. It went for $6,400. Then there is Edward Curtis's *The North American*

---

* Remarks delivered at *Art in America*'s symposium "Collecting the Photograph" (New York, Sept. 20, 1975).

† Lunn, op. cit.

Indian (*1907–1930*) with its 1,500 full-page photogravures. In eight months it soared in value from $11,000 to $60,000.

Steerage Sold for $4,500

Of all the most recent prices of note, however, the $4,500 paid for Stieglitz's *The Steerage* at Sotheby Parke Bernet in February, 1975, deserves special attention. Originally published in 1915 with volume 7–8 of *291,* the image achieved a record price for a twentieth-century photograph, or rather photogravure. A photogravure, instead of being made from a photographic negative, is created through a high-quality printing process using a metal plate. As such, even though gravures are by far the finest possible reproductions of photographs, "they are just not original photographs and should rather be compared to fine engravings made photographically on a copper plate and then printed with ink," according to Peter Pollack in *Popular Photography* magazine.*

So why the high price for a *Steerage*? First, because many people consider Stieglitz to be of inestimable importance to the entire "Photography is Art" movement. Second, because many people like *Steerage,* in direct opposition to others who find it boring and prefer other photographs by the artist. And third—and the most important factor for collectors intending to bid at an auction—because on the particular day that the particular $4,500 *Steerage* sold, at least two people in the room were willing to bid it up that high.

If one of them had not been there, it might have gone for much less, which indeed it did subsequently. At Sotheby Parke Bernet on September

* Pollack, Peter, "Photo-Print Prices: Onward and Upward," *Popular Photography* (Oct., 1975), p. 58.

GRANT MUDFORD (1944–   ). *London,* 1974 (Light Gallery).

Mudford, an Australian, became fascinated by the U.S. and relocated here. Almost immediately, he was given a show at a leading gallery on Madison Avenue.

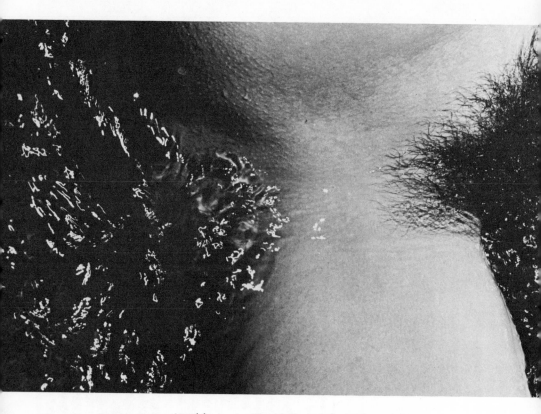

CHRIS ENOS (1944–   ). Untitled, 1974 (Enjay Gallery).

An element of mystery is usually missing from contemporary photographs of the nude female body. Not so in Enos' image of a woman, awash.

23, 1975, an admittedly not first-rate impression of the photograph fell to $2,800. It was a tumble that continues to puzzle many people. But Susan Harder of Light Gallery explains it by saying, "Everyone in that room who would want *Steerage* had one." Others insist that the bidding really hadn't stopped but that the auctioneer misunderstood and banged his gavel down too soon.

Photography Offers Few Authenticated Records

There are still a great many unexplained facts and figures in the photography marketplace to confuse speculators. It is a new field, one in which there are few authenticated records. No one knows, for instance, the exact number of photographs taken by any one photographer. Maybe 300 or 400 in the case of a Victorian. Over one million for living photographer Jay Maisel, or so he estimates. The problem is, no photographers have ever bothered to keep an *exact* count of their prints or color transparencies. Nor has anyone done the work for them. Nor do we know, in the majority of cases, precisely how many images a photographer may have printed of a particular image during his or her lifetime.

"We are still dealing in a vast never-never land," an expert admits. "Just about the time you think a particular photograph by a well-known artist has pretty much been bought up and therefore taken off the market, there's a new sale and still another one turns up. Someone, somewhere, read about the high price fetched for the photograph and they've remembered that they had 'one of those things' in their attic. Bang. Another print, or two, or three, hits the marketplace and we're off and running again, just as we thought we were nearing the finish line."

Hard to Consider Photography a Sure Investment

What this has done is to make photography more difficult to speak of definitely as an investment than almost any other art media, not to mention antiques. There are no irrefutable rules for collectors to abide by. Prices for some key works have gone up by as much as 1,000 percent. Others, as pointed out, have occasionally fallen. This will continue to happen. The marketplace today is unstructured. Unlike painting or furniture, which have had centuries of open-market sales from which investors and collectors can draw conclusions, photography has been sold regularly for only about five years, with the last two years the most active.

"And never forget," a collector says, "the prices the public pays a dealer are retail. Try to return a photograph for cash soon after you buy it and you'll be lucky if you get half what you paid for it. It may take you a while before you get back even what you paid for an image. And an auction takes from 12½ to 25 percent if you decide to sell that way. *But,* and this is an important but, if you're willing to wait five or six years, maybe less the way the marketing is going, chances are you'll be able to sell very well indeed."

Photographs by Young Artists Are Good Buys—but Rising

Of all the images on the market, though, those by contemporary photographers working today are probably among the best buys, and those with the greatest appreciation potential. Take, for example, a selection of one hundred photographs offered in the spring of 1976 by the Museum of Modern Art through its Art Lending Service. Presumably selected because of their aesthetic quality and therefore their collectability, the photographs were done by sixty-four artists, the majority of whom are well known, and sufficiently productive that they will soon build up a large enough body of work to create an active market for their images. Of the one hundred photographs, only twenty-six were priced over $500, and twelve were $150 or less. The majority were in the $200 to $400 range.

Two or three years ago, however, these same well-known artists' works were frequently priced as low as $50 to $75. With the rise in prices for nineteenth- and early-twentieth-century photographers' works, there has been an equivalent upward pull in contemporary photography prices as well. Today photographers who have traditionally had to fight to earn a living are able to earn handsome incomes through their gallery sales.

Extras Add to Value of Photograph

It should be recognized by collectors, though, that not all the works by a photographer are worth the same amount. Especially with deceased photographers, there can be certain aspects of a particular photograph that will often single it out from others by the same photographer and make it more desirable, therefore more expensive. An example would be a rare Edward S. Curtis portrait, *Geronimo,* a signed platinum print, 15½ by 12 inches, taken in 1905 when the famous Indian chief was a prisoner at

LEWIS BALTZ (1945–   ). *Construction Detail*, Santa Ana, 1975 (Castelli Graphics).

Baltz, one of the currently popular "Topographical Photographers," alerts us to the beauty and balance in construction sites and industrial parks. He proves that successful images are dependent upon perception, not subject matter.

Fort Sill, Oklahoma. Offered by the Robert Schoelkopf Gallery in 1975 for $2,000, it was twice as much as the gallery's copy of Curtis's *At the Well, Acoma,* a far better known, more prevalent print. A Man Ray of Gertrude Stein and Alice B. Toklas in their drawing room at 27 Rue de Fleurus in 1922, signed and dated by the photographer and inscribed to "Kitty Lou" by both sitters, was priced at $3,000 in the same catalog— while a portrait of Picasso by Man Ray taken in 1933 was tagged at $5,000 at Knoedler's a year later in a show where one Margaret Bourke-White was $300 (*RCA Speakers*) and another $600 (*Fort Peck Dam, Montana*).

Why the price ranges? Extras—such as famous people, fascinating locations, rarity, bizarre happenings, signatures—these almost fourth-dimensional aspects of some photographs add to their cost, and presumably will continue to distinguish the work and therefore accelerate its value.

Avoid Inferior Prints

Scratches, stains, and fading are to be guarded against, though. When equivalent images in better condition can be obtained, collectors should buy them. They will always command higher prices, but their resale value will be proportionally higher as well.

It is also wise to shop around when you are looking for a particular image you like. There are no regulated prices in the photography market, as pointed out. Auctioneers, dealers, antique shops, private collectors: with rare exceptions, everyone wants to get as much as they can for their photographs. But some ask, or are able to get, more than others. For instance, the day a *Steerage* sold for $4,500 at Sotheby Parke Bernet, Helios Gallery had an equivalent-quality photogravure of the same thing for more than $1,000 less. "Obviously, whoever bought their *Steerage* at auction hadn't done any sleuthing beforehand," says Scott Elliot.

It takes time and leg work to compare photograph prices, but, as demonstrated, the saving can be considerable! Enough to buy another photograph, quite often.

Also, collectors should know that auctions in the United States and abroad, which now sell over $1 million worth of photographs a year, are sometimes outlets for dealers and galleries to unload images they haven't been able to sell. Frequently they are photographs of less than premier quality. "But that isn't to diminish the value of auctions. It is only to alert people to facts which can sometimes be true," advises a cautious collector. "There can be wonderful things which come up at auctions, too."

Hidden Treasures

In fact, there was one miracle on Madison Avenue very recently. In 1976 at an auction of Sotheby Parke Bernet, lot 63 was described in the catalog as an 1869 photograph of Lucretia Coffin Mott, an activist in the anti-slavery and women's rights movement. Also part of the same lot (it is not an uncommon practice at auctions to offer several things for sale together if none of them is thought important) were two small photographic portraits by the Langenheim brothers. Barely mentioned in the catalog, they were explained as 1935 copies of original nineteenth-century calotype prints of these early pioneers in American photography. The estimated selling price of the three photographs was between $100 and $200.

DENNIS HEARNE (1947–   ). *Rutherford,* 1971 (Collection of the artist).
Primitive in its simplicity, Hearne's photograph *Rutherford* is a successful blend of charm, light, and texture. Gut reaction to an image frequently influences a collector's decision to buy. Fame isn't the only criterion.

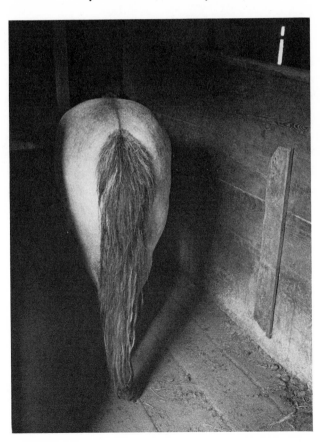

Bidding began at $100, climbed to $200. Then, when the audience thought the gavel would fall, someone raised the bid to $300, then $400, then $500. A hush fell on the room. Obviously at least two people in the room knew more than everyone else, the crowd realized. One of the bidders was Sam Wagstaff, the other was an unidentified dealer. Still the price rose. $800. $1,000. Finally Wagstaff won lot 63 for $1,900.

What was so important about the Mott portrait? astonished friends wanted to know afterward. Nothing at all, Wagstaff explained. It wasn't *her* photograph that he was after. It was the two images by the Langenheim brothers. They weren't copies. They were the real things, dating from about 1849, and signed by the two men on the back. Wagstaff had turned the photos over and seen the signatures. The auction house and most of the people in the room had not! Extremely valuable examples of early paper photography in America, the portraits had, in fact, appeared in an early history book on photography.

Edwin H. Land and the Polaroid

An important photographic development had also appeared in print in 1929 in Dick Calkin's cartoon strip. Somewhere in space, Buck Rogers needed a photo of himself to transmit to headquarters on earth. Complying, the hero sent a portrait of himself via ultraviolet television, to be self-developed and peeled off in seconds. Science fiction? Only for a while. In 1947 Edwin H. Land unveiled a brand-new device that did exactly what Buck Rogers had done. Land had seen the facts that allowed him to produce instantly processed pictures: that is, the Polaroid.

Today the question is: To what extent will the public see the facts in order to make photographs truly collectable? Many people already have. Will more? Yes. It is our belief that each succeeding year will bring more collectors into the photography marketplace. There is still a great deal of educating to do, though. It cannot be denied that the uncertainty of the infinitude of the negative remains the principal stumbling block. Despite efforts to set the record straight, the general public has still not accepted the fact that while it isn't unusual for an edition of a graphic print to number into the hundreds, maybe thousands, it is very rare for more than a handful of photographs to be made from one negative.

In time this will be better understood. Also, photographers may on occasion follow other artists' marketing techniques. Print-makers either damage or destroy their stones or plates. They do this so that they cannot be used again, thus assuring scarcity and therefore increasing value to their prints. Or they restrike an image, thus maintaining a value for their work but in varying degrees. While such processes are currently anathemas to most photographers who consider the preservation of their negatives as vital as the health of their heart, lungs, and kidneys, a few may be persuaded to follow suit. In the meantime, a few savvy photography enthusiasts aren't holding back. Time, they realize, isn't standing still. "Two years ago, I had plenty of great material, and not enough customers. . . . Now I have customers and I have a hard time finding the same quality material I had two years ago," says Helios' Scott Elliot. "The material simply isn't around any more. I had P. H. Emerson platinum prints and I had great Camerons and I had Steichens, and so on. When people want to buy now, I don't have a great deal to sell. It's not impossible to get them. Only harder. There is not enough material to supply the current demand." *

George Rinhart Buys 400,000 Photographs a Year

One of the reasons may be that of wholesaler/retailer George Rinhart, who is on record as having said, "Photography is the last frontier of graphic art. Sooner or later, original photographs by classic artists will be almost impossible to find. That's why I'm buying about 400,000 photographs a year, and holding on to about 200,000." †

A word to the wise is sufficient. Despite the hand-wringing, there are still a good many good nineteenth-century photographs available. And even though most are accelerating in price, so are a dozen eggs each

* Deschin, Jacob, "The Print Prospectors," *35-MM* (Spring, 1976), p. 70.

† "Think Positive, Photographs Have Emerged As a Promising New Speculation," *Barrons* (July 12, 1976), p. 19.

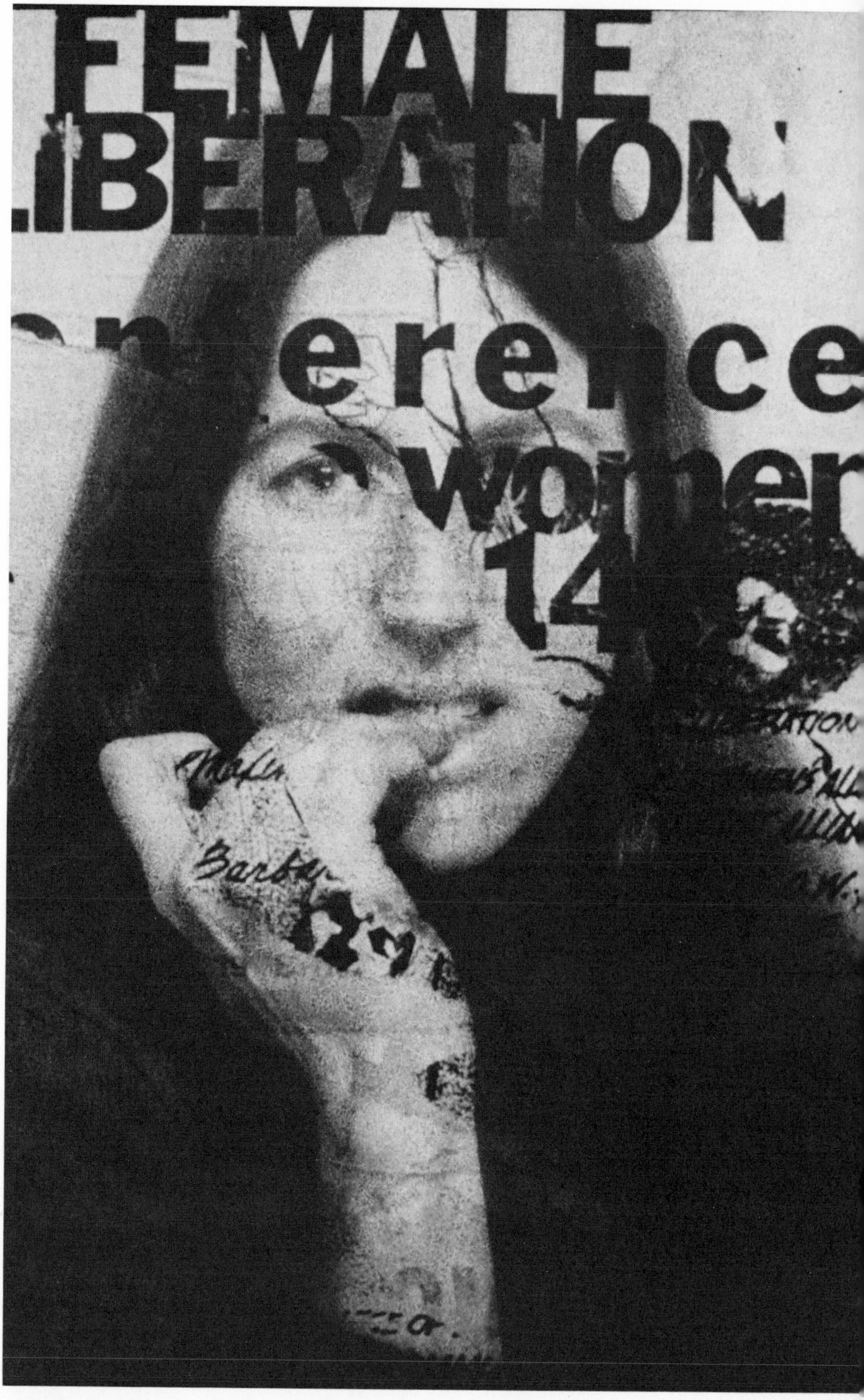
FEMALE
IBERATION

week. No one should be surprised anymore by higher costs. As for contemporary photography, it's still a buyer's market. The great masters of tomorrow are right here among us today. Collectors with vision will find them. Collectors with Wall Street aims will corner their works.

Rules for Investing in Art, Including Photography

With prices rising in all the arts—a Norman Rockwell painting worth $750 five years ago sells for $20,000 today; an abstract painting by Robert Brown that sold for $800 in 1973 was worth $4,000, or 400 percent more, three years later—anyone who is considering buying photographs for reasons other than personal aesthetics might like a review of some time-tested rules for art appreciation. "Appreciation" in dollars and cents, that is. Here is a list of suggestions:

Always Buy the Best. John Szarkowski of the Museum of Modern Art stresses the need to "start with the best pictures you can find, not only because they are fine, but because they set a standard of seriousness. But the best does not mean the most famous or the most predictable. The process of discovery in photography is by no means over. . . . So much that is exciting and excellent and that will be easily lost is still close at hand and readily available."

If there is a choice between three or four lesser prints at $150 apiece and one truly outstanding photograph at $450, buy the more expensive single image. The best art always appreciates the most. It is true with antiques and paintings, and it is becoming increasingly a rule in photography collecting, too.

Stay Away from Fads. Passing fads are a pitfall. Photography sales haven't yet occurred frequently enough to give many examples of stagnation or downfall in price. But paintings tell a tale. For instance, Amer-

---

BOBBI CAREY (1947–   ). *Consciousness Raising,* 1975 (Neikrug Gallery).

During 1975 and 1976, the self portrait became an ethic in the photography world, especially among women photographers. Carey's are among the more thought provoking.

ican Hudson River School painters reached a high point in 1971 and then stayed there! On the other hand, the Ashcan School is experiencing a steady rise. The thing to beware of the most is what happened to eighteenth-century English portrait painters, who were the rage of the 1920s. "People paid astronomical prices for them; in fact, they paid much more than they could ever hope to recover now," says Rupert Funnell of Sotheby Parke Bernet in Los Angeles.

Look for a Signature. Even now, signed photographs go for more than those without a John Hancock. It may be the difference will grow greater. It is certainly true with paintings. A Winslow Homer unsigned watercolor on paper sells for $20,000 to $25,000. At the same time, one that carries the artist's name, written in his own hand, demands $55,000 to $60,000 today. Therefore always buy an authentically signed photograph when you can.

Pay Attention to the Subject Matter. Subject matter is also something that a collector who is also an investor must be alert to. The public has certain favorites. Landscapes are one of them. A John Singer Sargent portrait in oil often commands only an $18,000 price, while the great painter's landscapes frequently sell for more than $50,000.

Study the Market. Find out how long the photographer in whose work you're interested has been producing images. How much they produce a year for sale. Whether they are popular with only a small number of fans, or whether they have a broader, perhaps even an international market. Production produces a market for an artist's works, and this makes investment in his creations viable.

Bargain Hard. If you feel sure of a photographer and he isn't gallery-represented, don't hesitate to buy. Chances are, in fact, that you'll save money if you go to him before he commits himself to a dealer. Some dealers take only a 40 percent commission from their artists. Most take 50 percent, though. If you go to a dealer, the more you spend, the more likely you can bargain. Also be certain to comparative-shop, making sure you have looked up the latest auction prices for any photographer you particularly like. Galleries can overprice. It's up to you to call their bluff.

JOHN DIVOLA (1949–   ). *Vandalism,* 1974 (Collection of the Fogg Art Museum).

Did he or didn't he spray the room himself? Whether or not Divola did, the paint splotches in this vandalized corner seem to float in space, creating an unusual image.

Hang Loose. Nobody, including art collectors, is perfect. And most investors do make mistakes, too. So when you know you've chosen badly —sell. Then buy again. But if you are after *really* meaningful financial appreciation, you will probably have to hang on to your choices three to five years. But whenever you do decide to sell, remember it may take a while. Three months isn't an excessive length of time to find a buyer.

Art can have very slow liquidity. It is one of the reasons that many investors prefer stocks and bonds.

Before You Buy, Get the Facts. Ask a dealer if you can return a print and receive the same price you paid for it up to a year later, or at least receive credit equivalent to the price you paid that can be applied to other photographs in the gallery. Some dealers permit you to buy on credit, normally 25 percent down with up to six months to pay the balance. Also ask for a guarantee of authenticity for the photograph you are buying. Collectors should not only ask themselves *why* they are purchasing an image, but they have every right to ask others *what* they are laying out money for. Get the facts down in writing! Who took the picture? When was it done? Who printed it? Was it signed by the photographer or someone else authorized to do so? When was it signed? If it is a portfolio, then precisely what do the words "Limited Edition" mean? Ignorance is seldom bliss, especially when making any kind of investment. A reputable auction house will take back anything it has misrepresented. Top photography dealers will do the same.

In summary, what makes art a good investment has traditionally been the object's rarity, its creator's innovative qualities, and whether or not the artist carries a broad-based and respected reputation. All of these facts can be learned about any photographer—Dead or Alive. But there is still one important demand put on the collector who looks to photographs as an investment.

Aesthetic Judgment Essential

A good eye is essential, usually the result of training. Marksmen have it. They've developed an eagle's vision through strong nerves, determination, and practice. Photography hunters need to do the same. Dealers aren't infallible. Nor are critics. And neither are museum curators. In the end, the decision to buy or not to buy is yours to make.

If a photograph increases in value and you *want* to sell it, you have only yourself to thank for having been wise enough to have bought it. If it decreases, find out why first, then complain. You may have only yourself to blame. At the moment there are very few downs in a generally up photography marketplace. In fact, based on the increase in photography prices in the 1970s, a contemporary photography collection, bought wisely, could easily double, if not triple, in value in the next ten years.

But collectors with an enormous love for photographs will buy what they like and let the future value be damned. For that is what photography collecting should really be all about. No one who truly loves great photographs buys them only for dollar and cents appreciation. They buy photographs because their soul demands it. If an image goes up in value —wonderful. If it doesn't—so what? They bought the photograph because they wanted to look at it.

And that is exactly why the photographer took the picture in the first place. Like you, he liked what he saw. For a really happy marriage, the photographer's and the buyer's visions should agree.

Appendix I.

ANSWERS TO THE QUESTIONS MOST OFTEN ASKED BY NEWCOMERS TO PHOTOGRAPHY COLLECTING

The following is a brief rundown on the issues that are the most puzzling to newcomers to photography collecting. All of them are discussed in depth in this book. We hope this condensation will intrigue anyone sufficiently that he or she will then want to read the entire book in an honest desire to know more.

QUESTION: Are photographs legitimate art?

ANSWER: Yes. But they haven't always been considered as such. According to the dictionary, any body of work subject to aesthetic criticism—paintings, drawings, sculpture—is art. There has, nevertheless, been a 150-year-old battle waged about photography's legitimate status. Until the last few years, supporters have been loud but occasional. Also, there haven't been enough of them. With their retreat, the pendulum either stopped dead center or swung dramatically to the other side. Sufficient strength is now in the "Photography Is Art" movement, however, that collectors can feel quite safe joining the ranks. Museums, including the Metropolitan Museum of Art in New York, the Boston Museum of Fine Arts, Atlanta's High Museum of Art, and the New Orleans Museum of Art collect photographs. Corporations—Seagram's, IT&T, 3M Company—are buying photographs for their art collections, too. Publications such as *Artforum* and *The Print Collector's Newsletter* now critique the photo scene. Newspapers, including *The New York Times* and *The Washington Post; Time* and *Newsweek;* television, including NBC's *Today Show*: they have all covered the topic of photography's current promotion by art dealers throughout the world.

QUESTION: Who says photographs are a good investment?

ANSWER: No one in particular, but a lot of people in general now recognize that the purchase of photographs is a good way to hang art on your walls and at the same time put money in the bank. The best-known photographers from the past—Julia Margaret Cameron, Nadar, Brady, those listed in the indexes of the major photography history books—are the blue-chip image-makers. Their work will undoubtedly appreciate in value the most. But lesser-known young photographers who are out shooting today should not be overlooked. Some of them will be considered great masters one day, too. Perhaps the greatest sign of the current times is the entry of the Original Print Collectors Group into the photography marketplace. Established primarily as a way for investors to capitalize on art's increase in value, the company has spotted the five-year rise of works by such photographers as Ansel Adams, from $150 to over $800; Walker Evans, from $160 to over $1,000; and Paul Strand, from $200 to as much as $12,000. Undoubtedly more attention will now be given to the investment incentive in first-quality photographs than ever before.

QUESTION: Isn't there a problem of a negative? Can't a photographer print thousands of copies of a picture and flood the marketplace?

ANSWER: Yes, he could, provided he wanted to spend several thousands of hours in his darkroom. Why doesn't he? Because photographers for the most part prefer gathering fresh material to standing in a hot, stuffy little room with their hands submerged in chemicals. Or they prefer to print lesser-known images than to keep on printing the same images that the public is mesmerized by. "With most photographers, it would be easier if you asked them to send you one of their fingers than to ask them to send you another one of their prints," says Harold Jones, head of Tucson's Center for Creative Photography. But even with the most popular image (other than a photogravure) ever personally printed by a photographer, Ansel Adams's *Moonrise, Hernandez,* the total number of prints in existence is still small. According to Adams, he has printed about 350 of this well-known image. Says the photographer, "We can print thousands of prints from a negative, but in truth, most negatives are represented by one print. . . ."

Of all the graphic arts, fewer prints are probably ever made from any photographic negative than from any printer's stone or plate. It is a fact still not generally known to the public. Nor are the reasons back of it sufficiently publicized. But as collectors wake up to the facts, the rarity of most photographs will be more appreciated and their prices will climb still faster.

QUESTION: Where do photographs come from?

ANSWER: From photographers. For many newcomers, it is baffling where dealers and museums find all the beautiful images they hang on their walls and hide in their drawers. But their sources aren't so mysterious. Living photographers' works are gotten by dealers directly from their creators, or through other dealers. There are wholesale photography dealers just as there are wholesale dry goods merchants or wholesale grocers. And there are auctions, antique shops, and flea markets that often sell nineteenth-century and early twentieth-century photographs. Also, many a photographer's family has held on to a photographer's negatives and prints out of a sense of loyalty. Today dealers spend a good deal of time ferreting out these buried treasures.

QUESTION: Why isn't a photograph of a photograph collectable?

ANSWER: For the same reason that a photograph of a Picasso, a Vermeer, or an Etruscan wall painting isn't the real thing. Taking a photograph is only the first step in a photographer's work. The printing of the negative is the real essential, the "telling" ingredient in the finished product. The choice of paper, the size of the print, the richness of color tone, the photographer's signature, an anecdote about the image in his own handwriting: there are countless "X" factors that make a genuine photograph personally printed by the artist the demanding collector's choice. The greatest possible creative input by the artist as well as his personal verification that it is his work: this combination makes the most valuable art items, including photographs.

QUESTION: What photographs should I buy?

ANSWER: Ask yourself first, "Am I buying for pure visual pleasure? Or am I buying for investment purposes only? Or am I buying for aesthetics *and* capital appreciation?" You've got to know which game you're playing in order to know which rules to abide by. But before you make any decisions, immerse yourself in photography books. Go to exhibitions at galleries and museums. Read books on the history of photography. There are styles of photography, techniques of printing, vast differences in subject matter. Become familiar with them all. Beginners often do well to pick a theme and collect images that pertain to it: western landscapes, urban poverty, bathing beauties of the 1920s. Specialization tends to refine the eye. It also builds up a collection frequently more fascinating than those selected through random sampling.

QUESTION: Where do I buy photographs?

ANSWER: For the newcomer, an art gallery that either includes or deals exclusively in photography is normally the first destination on an itinerary. There are over 125 galleries in the United States and over 75 in Europe that qualify at this time, to say nothing of exhibitions of photographers' work put on by camera clubs, photographers' cooperative galleries, and camera manufacturers.

But check on the reputation of any gallery with museum curators, art publication editors, fellow collectors. Many art galleries that sell photographs have been around for years; they've established their reputation for honesty. But many photography galleries are newcomers. Make sure you're a wise owl and not a dumb bunny when you go out to buy. So far there have been no serious customer complaints. But as the volume of photograph sales increases, it stands to reason there'll be more outlets. You don't have to be a Latin scholar to understand the importance of *caveat emptor*!

QUESTION: What is the extent of the photography market right now?

ANSWER: Smaller than the press would have readers believe. It is estimated that there are many occasional buyers, but only about forty aggressive private collectors in the photography marketplace today, few of whom spend more than $50,000 a year on images. The auctions in Europe and the United States do roughly $1 million a year in photograph sales—small potatoes compared to furniture, oriental rugs, and paintings. But remember that five years ago New York, which now has over thirty galleries handling photographs, had only two or three that dealt with photographic prints. It is the expectation that the art world has for photographs that is the real news of the market right now. As more print connoisseurs shift to photographs, or increase their willingness to include them in their collections, the larger the market is going to be.

QUESTION: Do I dare buy unfamous photographers' work?

ANSWER: Of course you do. Again, though, a lot depends on your intentions. If you simply want to own photographs because you love the medium, then buy exactly what you like and you'll be happy. Even if a person took only one gripping photograph in his or her lifetime, if you want it—get it. *But,* if you intend to collect and invest at the same time, then buy "names." People are still sufficiently insecure about photography that the well-known photographers will continue to climb the highest on the price ladder for a while. If you're gutsy, though, a $150 investment in a print by a young photographer who is definitely on the way to recognition *may* appreciate in value faster than $1,000 in a tried-and-true old-timer. But courage is essential if you plan to swim out from shore.

QUESTION: How do I know if a photograph is genuine or fake?

ANSWER: So far there are no known cases of outright forgery in the photography marketplace. No one has gone out and taken pictures that look like those by Gustave Le Gray, Timothy O'Sullivan, or Steichen, then tried to pass them off as authentic. They've done this with famous Impressionist painters, of course, but then, the rewards were into the high hundreds of thousands. The financial incentives aren't great enough in relation to the penalties of dishonesty to merit criminal minds entering the photography area yet. There have, however, been some careless misattributions and a few questionable signatures. The real issue is "Who printed the image?" Get your facts verified in writing if you want to be 100 percent safe. For instance, to say that an image is "a Weston" doesn't promise the buyer that Edward Weston printed it. His son may have. Some other photographers never bothered to print their own negatives. It may not matter to you, and in some cases it may not matter to most people. But be sure you get your facts straight before you buy, not afterward.

QUESTION: Why do you hear a lot about some contemporary photographers and nothing about others?

ANSWER: The photography marketplace isn't that much different from show business. The more your work is seen, the more you're talked about and written about, the more you're in demand, the more you're talked and written about, the more you sell, the more you're . . . and so on. The photo launching pad today is a prominent museum or gallery show. Critics come. Articles appear. The photographer's images become the basis of a book. Collectors see them and start to buy. Like anyone in the arts, a photographer hopes for his "first break." Once it is achieved, and if all the dials on the computer function properly, the multiplier goes into effect. There are a lot of very good unknown photographers, both deceased and still working. There are also thousands of very talented unrecognized actors and actresses. Not everyone who shows up for audition lands a role. Nor can everyone hang on a museum's walls. It's sad—but true.

QUESTION: Who other than dealers can advise me about photographs?

ANSWER: Peter Bunnell, director of the Art Museum at Princeton University and a noted authority on photography, receives hundreds of queries from collectors each year. Remarkably enough, he answers them. Including some rather unusual ones.

"One day I got a call from someone who said, 'I want to buy a photograph by someone, but he's not in the history of photography.' I couldn't figure out what the woman was talking about at first," the director said. "Then it dawned on me. She meant Newhall's *History of Photography*. The names of all the great photographers aren't in the book, and it was the absence of the name of the photographer whose work she liked that bothered this woman. I took a chance and said to her, 'You want to buy a Frederick Sommer, don't you?' I knew Sommer wasn't in the book. 'Yes,' she said in amazement. 'He's the one.'

" 'And you're standing in a Madison Avenue telephone booth, aren't you? Somewhere near a dealer's,' I inquired further. And again she said that I was right. 'But what shall I do?' the woman went on.

" 'Buy it,' I said. Then I hung up."

Other museum directors and curators may be willing to help you decide on a photograph, too!

QUESTION: What about color photographs? Are they as collectable as black and white ones?

ANSWER: More than ever before. Until recently, the main stumbling block has been the tendency of color prints to fade and therefore to be a poor investment. Now, through technical improvements, color photographs—if they are properly printed and processed—have greater longevity. They may even have complete permanence if they're intelligently cared for. Time will tell.

The other mark against color photographs has been a traditional snub. Curators, dealers, collectors, and photographers themselves have turned their noses up at color. Black and white photographers have been thought to be more aesthetic, able to handle composition, mood, and tonality with greater finesse, and not to be sidetracked by "color for color's sake." Now, though, the mood is changing. People are beginning to recognize that color doesn't have to be garish and commercial, but can be subtle and artistic. Two galleries devoted exclusively to color photographs have opened in New York. And photographers such as Ansel Adams, who has traditionally worked in black and white, are beginning to experiment. Adams spent part of the summer of '76 shooting with a Polaroid. Andy Warhol did the same six years ago. In fact, an exhibition with some of his images was held at the Gotham Book Mart in New York at the time. To-day, though, the serious collector is more likely to go after color photographs that are either C prints or dye transfers. Their longevity is more likely.

QUESTION: Once you own some photographs, what do you do with them?

ANSWER: It seems hard to believe, but this is a common query directed at dealers. "A good many people are astonished when we reply, 'Hang them on your walls,' " one Madison Avenue gallery owner says. "You hang paintings and prints on your walls, don't you? Go ahead and do the same with great photographs." One of the nicest things about photographs, also, is that you can rotate your collection. Put up a group of images this month, then a different selection next month. Photographs were taken because the photographers were interested in what they saw. You should be, too. Even if you do buy a photo-graph as an investment, dont' put it under your bed. Learn to live with it. Who knows? You may never want to give it up!

Appendix II.

A SELECT READING LIST

To collect art of any kind, a collector needs to know its history. The more he knows, the sharper his eye, and the better his collection can become. Photography collecting is no different; therefore anyone who becomes truly serious will want to own *The History of Photography* by Helmut and Alison Gernsheim and *The History of Photography: From 1839 to the Present Day* by Beaumont Newhall. They are the current bibles of the medium. But there are many other important books on photography, and the following reading list gives their titles.

It should also be recognized that there are currently hundreds of books on individual photographers with illustrations of their work. Collectors will want to be familiar with these educational sources, too.

Where do you go to buy books on and about photographs if your local general bookstore can't help you? Museums, photo galleries, and university bookstores frequently stock them. But if you strike out, write Light Impressions Corp., Box 3012, Rochester, N.Y. 14614. They'll send you their extensive mail-order photo book catalog.

Ackley, Clifford. *Private Realties: Recent American Photography.* New York: New York Graphic Society, 1974.

Baier, Wolfgang. *A Source Book of Photography.* New York: Focal Press, 1964.

Beaton, Cecil and Buckland, Gail. *The Magic Image, The Genius of Photography from 1839 to the Present Day.* Boston: Little Brown, 1975.

Boni, Albert, ed. *Photographic Literature: An International Bibliographical Guide.* New York: Morgan & Morgan, 1962.

Braive, M. F. *Photography, A Social History.* New York: McGraw-Hill, 1966.

Castle, Peter. *Collecting and Valuing Old Photographs.* London: The Garnstone Press, 1973.

Coke, Van Deren, ed. *One Hundred Years of Photographic History.* Albuquerque: University of New Mexico Press, 1975.

Coke, Van Deren. *The Painter and the Photograph.* Albuquerque: University of New Mexico Press, 1967.

Doty, Robert. *Photo-Secession: Photography as a Fine Art.* Rochester, N.Y.: George Eastman House, 1960.

Emerson, Peter Henry. *Naturalistic Photography for Students.* New York: Arno Press, 1973.

Gassan, A. *Chronology of Photography, A Critical Survey of the History of Photography as a Medium of Art.* Athens, Ohio: Handbook Co., 1972.

Gernsheim, Helmut and Alison. *Creative Photography, 1826 to the Present.* Detroit: Wayne University, 1963.

Gernsheim, Helmut and Alison. *A Concise History of Photography.* New York: McGraw-Hill Book Co., 1969.

Green, Jonathan. *Camera Work: A Critical Anthology.* Millerton, New York: Aperture, 1973.

Howarth-Loomes, B. E. C. *Victorian Photography, An Introduction for Collectors and Connoisseurs.* New York: St. Martin's Press, 1974.

Jones, B. E., ed. *Encyclopedia of Photography.* New York: Arno, 1974.

Lyons, Nathan. *Photographers on Photography.* Englewood Cliffs, N.J.: Prentice-Hall for George Eastman House, Rochester, N.Y., 1966.

Lyons, Nathan. *Photography of the 20th Century.* Rochester, New York: George Eastman House, 1967.

Newhall, Beaumont. *The Daguerreotype in America.* New York: Duell, 1961.

Newhall, Beaumont. *Latent Image, The Discovery of Photography.* Garden City, New York: Doubleday, 1967.

Newhall, Beaumont and Nancy. *Masters of Photography.* New York: George Braziller, Inc., 1958.

Newhall, Beaumont. *On Photography: A Source Book of Photographic History in Facsimile.* Watkins Glen, N. Y.: Century House, 1956.

Newhall, Beaumont. *The History of Photography: From 1839 to the Present Day.* 4th ed., rev. New York: The Museum of Modern Art, 1964.

Pollack, Peter. *The Picture History of Photography.* Rev. ed. New York: Harry N. Abrams, Inc., 1969.

Rinart, F. and M. *American Daguerreian Art.* New York: Potter, 1967.

Scharf, Aaron. *Art and Photography.* Baltimore, Md.: Penguin, Rev. 1974.

Szarkowski, John. *The Photographer's Eye.* New York: Museum of Modern Art, 1966.

Szarkowski, John. *Looking at Photographs.* New York: Museum of Modern Art, 1973.

Taft, Robert. *Photography and the American Scene.* New York: Macmillan Co., 1938.

Editors of Time-Life Books. *Color.* Life Library of Photography. New York: Time-Life Books, 1970.

Editors of Time-Life Books, *Caring for Photographs.* Life Library of Photography. New York: Time-Life Books, 1972.

Editors of Time-Life Books. *Great Photographers.* Life Library of Photography. New York: Time-Life Books, 1971.

Editors of Time-Life Books. *Frontiers of Photography.* Life Library of Photography. New York: Time-Life Books, 1972.

Time-Life Books. *Photography.* New York: Time, Inc., 1966.

Wilhelm, Henry. *Preservation of Contemporary Photographic Material.* Grinnell, Iowa: East Street Gallery, 1976.

ADDITIONAL SOURCES OF INFORMATION

The following is a list of publications that either are devoted entirely to photography, photographs and photographers, or allocate a substantial portion of each issue to the photographic medium. Many are new. The current enthusiasm for collecting photographs has spurred magazine publishers into action just as it has lit a bonfire under book publishers. How do you know which publications you might like to subscribe to? Write a postcard and ask for a sample issue if you can't find a copy at a local newsstand, or in a museum or photo gallery bookstore.

Afterimage, Visual Studies Workshop, 4 Elton St., Rochester, N.Y. 14607

Art in America, 150 East 58th St., New York, N.Y. 10022

Art International, 45 Neuschelstrasse, 8001 Zurich, Switzerland

Art News, 750 Third Ave., New York, N.Y. 10017

Artforum, P.O. Box 980, Farmingdale, N.Y. 11735

Arts Magazine, 23 East 26th St., New York, N.Y. 10010

Aura, 493 Franklin St., Buffalo, N.Y. 14202

The British Journal of Photography, 24 Wellington St., London WC2E 7DH, England

Camera, c/o C. J. Bucher Ltd., CH-6002, Lucerne, Switzerland

Camera 35, 420 Lexington Ave., New York, N.Y. 10017

Creative Camera, 19 Doughty St., London WC12 2PT England

Document, 416 Park Ave., So., New York, N.Y. 10016

Fotofile, 492 Broome St., New York, N.Y. 10013

Fotografia Italiana, Via degli Imbriani 15, 20158 Milan, Italy

History of Photography, c/o Light Impressions Corp., P.O. Box 3012, Rochester, N.Y. 14614

Image, 900 East Ave., Rochester, N.Y. 14607

Modern Photography, 130 East 59th St., New York, N.Y. 10022

Museum News, 2223 Wisconsin Ave., N.W., Washington, D.C. 20007

The Philadelphia Photo Review, P.O. Box 70, Arcola, Pa. 19420

The Photo Reporter, 319 East 44th St., New York, N.Y. 10017

Photocinema, 189 Rue St. Jacques, Paris 8e, France

Photo-Forum, P.O. Box 10-163, Auckland 4, New Zealand

Photograph, 210 Fifth Ave., New York, N.Y. 10010

Photographer, P.O. Box 24954, Vancouver, B.C., Canada V5T 4G3

The Photographic Journal, 14 So. Audley St., London W1Y 5DP England

Picture Magazine, 3818 Brunswick Ave., Los Angeles, Calif. 90039

Popular Photography, 1 Park Ave., New York, N.Y. 10016

The Print Collector's Newsletter, 50 East 78th St., New York, N.Y. 10021

Printletter, Postfach 250, CH-8046 Zurich, Switzerland

Studio International, 14 W. Central St., London WC1A 1JH England

Zoom, 2 Rue de Faubourg Poissonière, 75010 Paris, France

Appendix III.

SOURCES OF CONSERVATIONAL SUPPLIES

Restorers and conservators have gained great expertise in working with paintings, furniture, lithographs, and other art media. But few people specialize in photography restoration and conservation. More are beginning to do so, though, including a few collectors. For them, the following list of suppliers of photographic material for the conservation of photographs should be helpful.

Frames
Kulicke Frames, Inc., 636 Broadway, New York, N.Y. 10012
Laden Frame Co., 1433 South Wabash, Chicago, Ill. 60605

General Suppliers
Aiko's Art Materials Import, 714 North Wabash Ave., Chicago, Ill. 60611
   (Japanese papers for mending and mat decoration)
S & W Framing Supplies, Inc., 1845 Highland Ave., New Hyde Park, N.Y. 11040
   (Tools for mat-cutting and framing; catalog available)
Talas, Div'n of Technical Library Service, 104 Fifth Ave., New York, N.Y. 10011

(All restoration and conservation supplies, including transparent mylar polyester sheet protectors, board, neutral pH interleaving glassine, tools, papers, etc.)

Washi No Mise, 64 Pioneer Street, Apt. B, Cooperstown, N.Y. 13326
(Japanese tools and brushes for applying pastes)

Special Papers and Mounting Board

Andrew/Nelson/Whitehead, 31-10 48th Avenue, Long Island City, N.Y. 11101
(Protective papers, decorative mat papers, all-rag museum board, etc.)

Charles T. Bainbridge's Sons, 808 Georgia Ave., Brooklyn, N.Y. 11207
(All-rag museum board, also distributor for Keeton Cutter for mats)

Frome Bord Service Center, 2211 North Elston Ave., Chicago, Ill. 60614
(Distributor of Monsanto's "Frome-Cor Board" for backing frames; also box fillers for print storage)

Process Materials Corp., 329 Veterans Blvd., Carlstadt, N.J. 07072
(All-rag museum and non-rag museum board, acid-free lining paper, and wrapping paper; methyl cellulose paste powder and promacto adhesive; catalog available)

Sorg Paper Company, 901 Manchester Avenue, Middletown, Ohio 45042
(Acid-free blotting paper)

Strathmore Paper Company, Broad St., Westfield, Mass. 01085
(All-rag museum board)

University Products, Inc., P.O. Box 101, South Canal St., Holyoke, Mass. 01040
(All-rag museum board)

Plexiglas

Rohm and Haas Company, 465 Boulevard, Elmwood Park, N.J. 07407
(Ultraviolet filtering Plexiglas)

Storage Containers for Prints

Hollinger Corp., 3810 South Four Mile Run Drive, Arlington, Va. 22206
(Storage containers; also Permalife acid-free papers for protecting print surfaces)

Pohlig Brothers, Inc., 2419 East Franklin Streets, Richmond, Va. 23223
(Custom-made storage containers)

Spink and Gaborc, Inc., 32 West 18th St., New York, N.Y. 10011
(Solander boxes and custom-made print containers)

Archival Supplies

East Street Gallery, 725 State St., Box 616, Grinnell, Iowa 50112
(Supplies for archivally processing photographs; catalog available)

Bookbinding Tapes for Mats

Demco Library Supplies, P.O. Box 1488, Madison, Wis.
(Linen tape)
Gane Brothers and Lane, Inc., 1400 Greenleaf, Elk Grove, Ill. 60007
(Holland cloth tape)

Appendix IV.
WHERE TO GO TO BUY AND TO
SEE PHOTOGRAPHS

A. PHOTOGRAPHY GALLERIES AND DEALERS IN THE UNITED STATES, CANADA, EUROPE, ASIA AND THE PACIFIC

Each month the list of art galleries and dealers handling photographs grows longer. While New York City has the greatest number, other large cities—and smaller towns—throughout the world now also offer collectors opportunities to buy photographs. The following list is as up to date as a publisher's deadline allows.

Hours and days of the week when galleries and dealers open their doors vary. Normally it is Tuesday through Saturday, 10 A.M. to 6 P.M. It should also be pointed out that the number of galleries and dealers that deal *exclusively* in photographs is minimal. Many handle paintings and graphics, as well.

But most of the galleries and dealers (some of whom, you'll notice, work only "By Appointment," so you must call ahead) maintain inventories of photographs, even when they aren't having a photo exhibition. Therefore, ask to see what they have in their back room, usually in big black boxes.

Galleries and dealers also take orders for a living photographer's prints if they haven't the particular ones you want in stock. The problem is, you may have to wait up to six months until the photographer finds the time to go into the darkroom!

215

U.S. Photo Galleries and Dealers.

CALIFORNIA

BAKERSFIELD

Photographic Gallery
211 H St.
93304

BERKELEY

Darkroom/Workshop
2051 San Pablo Ave.
94702

BEVERLY HILLS

Dream Gallery
2231 Benedict Canyon Dr.
90210

CARMEL

Friends of Photography
San Carlos and 9th Ave.
93921

Weston Photographic Gallery
Sixth Ave. and Dolores
93921

LAGUNA BEACH

Lang Photography Gallery
1450-A South Coast Highway
92651

LOS ANGELES

Betty Gold Gallery
723½ North La Cienega
90069

Camerawork & Soho Photo Galleries
8221 Santa Monica Blvd.
90046

James Corcoran Gallery
8223 Santa Monica Blvd.
90046

G. Ray Hawkins Gallery
9002 Melrose Ave.
90069

KFAC Skinny Art Gallery
5773 Wilshire Blvd.
90036

Los Angeles Art Assoc. Galleries
825 No. La Cienega Blvd.
90069

Los Angeles Photography Center
412 South Parkview St.
90057

Soho Photo Gallery
8221 Santa Monica Blvd.
90046

Nicholas Wilder Gallery
8225½ Santa Monica Blvd.
90046

NEWPORT BEACH

Jack Glenn Gallery
260 Newport Center Drive
92660

Susan Spiritus Gallery
3336 Via Lido
92663

SACRAMENTO

Library Gallery
E. B. Crocker Art Gallery
216 O St.
95814

SAN FRANCISCO

Camerawork
898 Folsom St.
94107

Focus Gallery
2146 Union St.
94123

Grapestake Gallery
2876 California St.
94115

Hansen-Fuller Gallery
228 Grant Ave.
94108

Highland Gallery
3216 Fillmore St.
94123

John Howell Books
434 Post St.
94102

Lawson Galleries
54 Kissling St.
94103

Lucas Gallery
2250 Union St.
94123

New Gallery Photographs
1027 Hayes St.
94117

Phoenix Gallery
257 Grant Ave.
94108

Thackrey & Robertson Gallery
2266 Union St.
94123

SANTA CRUZ

Gallery 115
115 Maple St.
95060

SANTA ROSA

Annex Photo Gallery
604 College Ave.
95404

SONOMA

Creative Eye Photo Gallery
414 First St. East

COLORADO

DENVER

Cosmopolitan Art Gallery
701 South Milwaukee St.
80209

CONNECTICUT

LITCHFIELD

The Photographers' Gallery
On-the-Green
06759

CONNECTICUT—Cont.

NEW CANAAN

Photo Graphic Workshop & Gallery
212 Elm St.
06840

NEW HAVEN

Archetype Photographic Gallery
159 Orange St.
06510

SOUTH WOODSTOCK

Charles B. Wood, III, Inc.
The Green
06281

DISTRICT OF COLUMBIA

Colorfax Photo Gallery
5511 Connecticut Ave., N.W.
20015

Lunn Gallery
3243 P St., N.W.
20007

Sander Gallery
2604 Connecticut Ave., N.W.
20008

Washington Gallery of Photography
216 Seventh St., S.E.
20003

FLORIDA

DE BARY

Frank D. Guarino
P.O. Box 89
32713

PALM BEACH

Gallery Gemini
245 Worth Ave.
33480

GEORGIA

ATLANTA

Fay Gold Gallery
533 Holldale Court, N.W.
30342

Nexus Gallery
1185 Virginia Ave., S.E.
30306

ILLINOIS

ARLINGTON HEIGHTS

Graphic Antiquity
P.O. Drawer 1234
60006

CHICAGO

ARC Gallery
226 East Ontario St.
60611

Jacques Baruch Gallery
900 N. Michigan Ave.
Suite 605
60611

The Darkroom
2424 North Racine Ave.
60614

Allan Frumkin Gallery
620 North Michigan Ave.
60611

Luba Galleries
2439 North Clark St.
60614

INDIANA

FORT WAYNE

Gallery 614
614 West Berry St.
46802

IOWA

GRINNELL

East Street Gallery
723 State St.
50112

LOUISIANA

NEW ORLEANS

Chama Institute
5717 Magazine
70115

Images Gallery
8124 Oak St.
70118

Soho Photo Gallery
134 Exchange Place
70130

MASSACHUSETTS

BOSTON

Enjay Gallery
35 Lansdowne St.
02139

Harcus Krakow Gallery
7 Newbury St.
02116

Panopticon Gallery
69 Newbury St.
02116

Photoworks
755 Boylston St.
02167

Stephen T. Rose
456 Beacon St.
02115

William L. Schaeffer
279 Beacon St.
02167

Siembab Gallery
162 Newbury St.
02116

Vision Gallery
216 Newbury St.
02116

CAMBRIDGE

Clarence Kennedy Gallery
770 Main St.
02139

The Photographic Eye
5 Boylston St.
02167

Prospect Street Photo Co-op & Gallery
188 Prospect St.
02139

MICHIGAN

ANN ARBOR

Art Worlds
213½ South Main Street
48104

BIRMINGHAM

The Halstead 831 Gallery
560 North Woodward
48011

MINNESOTA

MINNEAPOLIS

Peter M. David Gallery
920 Nicollet Mall
55402

MISSOURI

COLUMBIA

Columbia Gallery of Photography
1015 East Broadway
65201

ST. LOUIS

13 X 15 Photographic Gallery
118 East Lockwood
63119

NEW JERSEY

WESTFIELD

Inner Visions Gallery
520 South Avenue West
07090

NEW MEXICO

ALBUQUERQUE

Quivira Photograph Gallery
111 Cornell Drive S.E.
87106

SANTA FE

Gallery f/22
338 Camino del Monte Sol
87501

NEW YORK

BROOKLYN

Atlantic Gallery
81 Atlantic Ave.
11201

BUFFALO

CEPA Gallery
3230 Main St.
14209

NEW YORK CITY

Timothy Baum
(By appointment only)
40 East 78th St.
10021

Carlton Gallery
127 East 69th St.
10021

Castelli Graphics
4 East 77th St.
10021

Crossroads
2639 Broadway
10025

Discovery Gallery/Modernage
319 East 44th St.
10017

Floating Foundation of Photography
15 Greene St.
10013

Foto
492 Broome St.
10013

4th Street Gallery
67 East 4th St.
10003

Frederica Harlow Gallery, Inc.
1100 Madison Ave.
10028

Helios Gallery
18 East 67th St.
10021

Images, Inc.
11 East 57th St.
10022

International Center of
  Photography
1130 Fifth Ave.
10028

Sidney Janis Gallery
6 West 57th St.
10019

K & L Gallery
222 East 44th St.
10017

Kimmel/Cohn Photography Arts
41 Central Park West
10023

M. Knoedler & Co., Inc.
21 East 70th St.
10021

Janet Lehr
(By appointment only)
45 East 85th St.
10028

Light Gallery
724 Fifth Ave.
10019

Marcuse Pfeifer Gallery
825 Madison Ave.
10021

Marlborough Gallery
40 West 57th St.
10019

Meisel Gallery
141 Prince St.
10021

Midtown Y Gallery
344 East 44th St.
10017

Multiples, Inc.
55 East 80th St.
10021

Neikrug Gallery
224 East 68th St.
10021

Portogallo Gallery
72 West 45th St.
10036

NEW YORK—Cont.

Rinhart Galleries, Inc.
818 Madison Ave.
10021

Donna Schneier
(By appointment only)
251 East 71st St.
10021

Robert Schoelkopf Gallery
825 Madison Ave.
10021

Sequential Gallery
41 East 59th St.
10021

Soho Photo Gallery
34 West 13th St.
10011

Sonnabend Gallery
420 West Broadway
10012

Theatre Gallery
961 Madison Ave.
10021

Third Eye Photo Gallery
17 Seventh Ave. South
10014

Witkin Gallery
41 East 57th St.
10022

Zabriskie Gallery
29 West 57th St.
10019

ROCHESTER

Visual Studies Workshop Gallery
4 Elton St.
14607

OHIO

CLEVELAND

Nova Gallery
1290 Euclid Ave., Rm. 207
44115

EAST PALESTINE

Vista Gallery
164 S. Market St.
44413

OKLAHOMA

TULSA

Clubb Gallery
Philbrook Art Center
2272 S. Rockford
74114

OREGON

EUGENE

Pearl St. Gallery
410 Pearl St.
97401

PORTLAND

Blue Sky Photographic Gallery
2315 N.W. Lovejoy
97210

PENNSYLVANIA

BERWYN

The Photographic Place
885 Lancaster Ave.
19312

CHESTNUT HILL

Hahn Gallery
8439 Germantown Ave.
19118

PHILADELPHIA

Janet Fleisher Gallery
211 South 17th St.
19103

Photopia
1728 Spruce St.
19103

Soho Photo Gallery
162 No. 3rd St.
19106

STRAFFORD

The Photography Place
503 West Lancaster Ave.
19087

TEXAS

AUSTIN

Crystal Root Gallery
2307A Rio Grande
78705

DALLAS

Afterimage Gallery
The Quadrangle No. 151
2800 Routh St.
75201

HOUSTON

Cronin Gallery
2424 Bissonnet
77005

UTAH

SALT LAKE CITY

Edison Street Gallery
231 Edison St.
84111

VERMONT

PAWLET

Mr. and Mrs. Tom Burnside
(By appointment only)
05761

VIRGINIA

FAIRFAX

Fuller & Albert Gallery
3170 Campbell Drive
22030

RICHMOND

Scott-McKennis Fine Art
3465 West Cary St.
23221

WASHINGTON

SEATTLE

Photo Printworks
114 Elliott West
98119

TACOMA

Silver Image Gallery
727 Commerce St.
98402

WISCONSIN

MILWAUKEE

Infinite Eye Gallery
2553 No. Downer Ave.
53211

Canada

BRITISH COLUMBIA

VANCOUVER

Mind's Eye
52 Water St.

ONTARIO

TORONTO

Deja-Vue Photographic Gallery, Inc.
122 Scollard

Marlborough Godard Gallery
22 Hazelton Ave.

QUEBEC

MONTREAL

Galerie Yajima
1625 Oëst Rue Sherbrooke

QUEBEC

Galerie Optica
453 St. Francois Xavier

Europe

AUSTRIA

GRAZ

Fotogalerie im Forum Stadtpark
Stadtpark 1

Fotogalerie "Klo"
Prokopigasse 16/1

VIENNA

Galerie Die Brücke
Backerstrasse 5

BELGIUM

ANTWERP

Paule Pia Photo Galerij
Kammenstraat 57

BRUSSELS

Galerie Spectrum
15 Rue de la Chapelle

Galerie & Fils
105 Blvd. Brand Whitlock

Ilford Gallery
180 Terkamerenstraat

GHENT

Photogalerie 5.6
St. Michielsplein 14

DENMARK

COPENHAGEN

G. C. P. Fotografisk Galleri
Vesterfaelledvej 2

Gallery Huset
Magstraede 14

FRANCE

AGEN

Atelier 6
22 Rue Richard Cœur de Lion

BOLLWILLER

Nicéphore
8 Rue de la Gare

LYON

Galerie Delta
58 Rue de la Republique

PARIS

Agathe Gaillard
3 Rue de Pont-Louis-Philippe

Galerie Contrejour
19 Rue de l'Ouest

Galerie Delpire
13 Rue de l'Abbaye

Galerie Jean Dieuzaide
4 Place St. Etienne

Galerie Gerard Lévy
17 Rue de Beaune

Galerie La Tortue
11 Rue Jacob

Galerie Sonnabend
12 Rue Mazarine

La Photogalerie
2 Rue Christine

Zabriskie Gallery
29 Rue Aubry Le Boucher

RENNE

Galerie Upsilone
5 Rue St-Michel

GERMANY (West)

AACHEN

Fotogalerie Lichttropfen
Kockerellstrasse 19

BERLIN

Galerie Mikro
Carmerstrasse 1

Galerie A. Nagel
Markelstrasse 46

Trockenpresse
Schluterstrasse 70

GERMANY (West)—Cont.

COLOGNE

Galerie Jollenbeck
Lindenstrasse 18

Galerie Wilde
Försterstrasse 27

ESSEN-KETTWIG

Galerie im Riek
Ruhrstrasse 44

HAMBURG

Galerie Levy
Magdalenenstrasse 26

Photogalerie
Kielerstrasse 171

Fotogalerie f/32
Erikastrasse 89

HANNOVER

Galerie Spectrum
Holzmarkt 6

Galerie Z
Silberstrasse 30

KIEL

Fotogalerie Nune
Masseldieksdammer Uleg 9

LEVERKUSEN

Agfa-Gevaert A.G.

MUNICH

Galerie Arnoldi-Livie
Maximilianstrasse 36

Galerie Walter Kober
Leopoldstrasse 13

STUTTGART

Gallerie im Kettenladle
Paulinenstrasse 53

Kunstkabinett G.A. Richter
Konigstrasse 33

GREAT BRITAIN

BRISTOL

Arnolfini Gallery
W'shed Canons Road

LONDON

Anderson & Hershkowitz Ltd.
90 Wigmore St.

Russ Anderson
59 Montholme Rd.

Box Room of Photography
125 Shaftsbury Avenue

Colnaghi's
14 Old Bond St.

Creative Camera Gallery
19 Doughty St.

Half Moon Gallery
27 Alie St.

Howard Ricketts Ltd.
180 New Bond St.

Marlborough Fine Arts
6 Albemarle St.

The Photographers' Gallery
8 Great Newport St.

YORK

Impressions Gallery of Photography
39 The Shambles

ITALY

BERGAMO

Galleria dell'Immagine
Piazza Vecchia 4

MILAN

Galleria Il Diaframma
Via Brera 10

Luciano Inga-Pin
Via Pontaccio 12/A

PISA

Galleria Fotografica Nadar
Vicolo dei Tidi 26

NETHERLANDS

AMSTERDAM

Galeri Fiolet
Herengracht 86

Canon Photo Gallery
Reestraat 19

POLAND

WARSAW

Union of Polish Art Photographers
Plac Zamkowy 8

SPAIN

BARCELONA

Spectrum Art Photographic Gallery
Balmes 86

MADRID

La Photo Galeria
Płaza de la Republica Argentina, 2

SWEDEN

MALMÖ

Malmö Konsthall
Johannesgatan 7

STOCKHOLM

Fotografiecentrum
Malmskillnadsgatan 45

SWITZERLAND

BASEL

Galerie Handschin
Baumleingasse 16

Photo Art
St. Albans–Vorstadt 10

CAROUGE

Galerie de Photographie
25 Rue de Pont-Neuf

GENEVA

Galerie Sonnabend
14 Rue Etienne-Dumont

Galerie Rivolta
1 Rue de la Mercerie

SWITZERLAND—Cont.

Soft Art Galerie
31 Rue Centrale

Galerie 38
Kirchgasse 38

ZURICH

Claudia Tadini
Clausuisstr. 64

Gallery Tolgge
Juggenhaus
Wasserwerk Str. 17

Photogalerie Kunsthaus Zurich
Heimplatz 1

Picture Gallery
Fortunagasse 20

YUGOSLAVIA

LJUBLJANA

Fotogalerija Focus
Podhod Zvezda

Asia and Pacific

AUSTRALIA

MELBOURNE

Brummels Gallery of Photography
95 Toorak Road
South Yarra

SYDNEY

Hogarth Galleries
7–9 McLaughlan Place
Paddington

JAPAN

TOKYO

Eikoh Hosoe
5 Aizumi-cho, Shinjuku-ku

Nantenshi Gallery
3–11 Kyobashi
Chuo-ku

B. AUCTION HOUSES THAT SELL PHOTOGRAPHS IN THE UNITED STATES AND EUROPE

The regular sale of any category of art at the world's most important auction houses is a sign that the art medium has arrived. Thus it can be said that photography is now a major collectable. In 1976 the sale of photographic prints at auctions in Europe and the United States topped $1 million.

The following is a list of the auction houses that sell photographs, often several times a year. Before a sale, an exhibition of the prints is normally held for two or three days to allow prospective bidders to examine the works.

Leading auction houses "stand behind" their sales. If they list a photograph in a catalog one way and you find out they were wrong and can prove it, you'll usually get your money back. But without interest, of course!

Bidding by mail is also possible, but not advisable. It's always better to be at an auction if you intend to buy. Fortunately New York City auction houses that sell photographs schedule their sales one day after another in the same week each spring and fall. This allows collectors who fly in from all over the world an easy opportunity to attend them all.

If you write to the auction houses, they will send you their photography sale catalogs ahead of time—but for a price.

United States

CALIFORNIA

SAN FRANCISCO

California Book Auction Company
224 McAllister St.

NEW YORK

NEW YORK

Martin Gordon Gallery, Inc.
25 East 83rd St.

Sotheby Parke Bernet, Inc.
980 Madison Avenue

Swann Galleries, Inc.
104 East 25th St.

Europe

ENGLAND

LONDON

Sotheby's Belgravia
19 Motcomb St.

Christie's
85 Old Brompton Rd.

C. MUSEUM AND LIBRARY COLLECTIONS IN THE UNITED STATES, CANADA, AND EUROPE

There is no better way to learn to appreciate fine photographs than to hold them in your hand, to have the time and permission to look at them at leisure. Print study rooms of museums and libraries often have important photographs available for the public to examine. However, an appointment is usually necessary since these rooms and their staffs are small. It is therefore recommended that a collector telephone ahead to the following museums and libraries to determine the nature and extent of their collections and when they may be seen.

United States

ALABAMA

Birmingham Museum of Art

Montgomery Museum of Fine Arts

ARIZONA

Center for Creative Photography
The University of Arizona
Tucson

CALIFORNIA

Bancroft Library
University of California
Berkeley

Los Angeles County Museum of Art

Oakland Museum

San Francisco Art Institute

DISTRICT OF COLUMBIA

Corcoran Gallery of Art

Library of Congress

National Archives

Smithsonian Institution

GEORGIA

High Museum of Art
Atlanta

Columbus Museum of Arts and Crafts

ILLINOIS

Art Institute of Chicago

INDIANA

Art Gallery
University of Notre Dame
South Bend

KANSAS

Museum of Art
University of Kansas
Lawrence

LOUISIANA

New Orleans Museum of Art

MARYLAND

University of Maryland Library
Baltimore County
Baltimore

MASSACHUSETTS

Addison Gallery of American Art
Phillips Academy
Andover

Museum of Fine Arts
Boston

Fogg Art Museum
Harvard University
Cambridge

Worcester Art Museum

MINNESOTA

Minneapolis Institute of Arts

MISSOURI

William Rockhill Nelson Gallery of
    Art and Atkins Museum of
    Fine Arts
Kansas City

NEW JERSEY

Princeton University Art Museum
Princeton

NEW MEXICO

Art Museum
University of New Mexico
Albuquerque

NEW YORK

Albright-Knox Art Gallery
Buffalo

International Center of Photography
New York City

Metropolitan Museum of Art
New York City

Museum of Modern Art
New York City

New-York Historical Society
New York City

International Museum of Photography
George Eastman House
Rochester

Everson Museum of Art
Syracuse

TEXAS

Art Museum
University of Texas
Austin

Amon Carter Museum of Western Art
Fort Worth

Museum of Fine Arts
Houston

VIRGINIA

Virginia Museum of Fine Arts
Richmond

WASHINGTON

Seattle Art Museum
Fine Arts Gallery
Cheney Cowles Memorial Museum
Spokane

WEST VIRGINIA

Huntington Galleries

Canada

OTTAWA

National Gallery of Canada

Europe

AUSTRIA

VIENNA

Graphische Lehr und
    Versuchsanstalt

DENMARK

COPENHAGEN
The Royal Library

FINLAND

HELSINKI
Finska Fotografiska Museet

FRANCE

CHALON-SUR-SAÔNE
Musée Nicéphore Niépce

PARIS

Bibliothèque Nationale

Librairie Paul Jammes

Musée Carnavalet

Société Française de la
    Photographie

TOULOUSE

Galerie Muncipale du
    Château d'Eau

GERMANY

HAMBURG
Staatliche Landesbildstelle

MARBURG
Staatliche Lichtbildstelle

GREAT BRITAIN

ABERDARE, GLAMORGAN
Public Library

BIRMINGHAM
Birmingham Public Library

EDINBURGH
Public Library
Royal Scottish Museum
Scottish National Portrait Gallery

HARROW
Kodak Museum

KINGSTON-UPON-THAMES
Public Library

LACOCK
Fox Talbot Museum

LONDON
British Museum
Greater London Council
Guildhall Library
Hayward Gallery
Imperial War Museum
London Museum
National Maritime Museum
National Portrait Gallery
Royal Academy of Arts
Royal Geographical Society

Royal Photographic Society of
Great Britain
Science Museum
Victoria and Albert Museum

OXFORD
Bodleian Library

READING
Museum of English Rural Life

WHITBY
Sutcliffe Gallery

ITALY

TURIN
Museo del Cinema

NETHERLANDS

LEIDEN
Leiden University Library

SWEDEN

STOCKHOLM
Fotografiska Museet

SWITZERLAND

ZURICH
Kunstgewerbemuseum

INDEX

234